# THE SINKING OF THE SCHARNHORST

D0596478

Corvette-Captain
Fritz-Otto Busch

# The Sinking Of
# The Scharnhorst

A factual account from the German viewpoint

Translated from the German by Eleanor Brockett
and Anton Ehrenzweig

Futura Publications Limited

A Futura Book

First published in Great Britain in 1956
by Robert Hale Limited
First Futura Publications edition 1974
This book was originally published under the title
THE DRAMA OF THE SCHARNHORST

ISBN 0 8600 71308
Printed in Great Britain by
C. Nicholls & Company Ltd.
The Philips Park Press
Manchester.

Futura Publications Limited,
49 Poland Street,
LONDON W1A 2LG

TO THE MEMORY OF THE GALLANT DEAD
OF THE BATTLESHIP *SCHARNHORST*

# CONTENTS

|  | *Foreword* | *page* 11 |
|  | *Introduction* | 13 |
| I | Biography of a Battleship | 15 |
| II | The Naval and Military Situation in 1943 | 42 |
| III | "J.W. Convoy en route for Murmansk" | 47 |
| IV | The *Scharnhorst* puts to Sea | 51 |
| V | The Royal Navy and the Convoys | 72 |
| VI | The British Radar Apparatus | 76 |
| VII | Admiral Sir Bruce Fraser sets the Trap | 79 |
| VIII | The *Duke of York* sails with Force 2 | 83 |
| IX | The Net is Cast | 86 |
| X | The *Scharnhorst* on her Sortie | 91 |
| XI | Vice-Admiral Burnett attacks with the 10th Cruiser Squadron, Force 1 | 103 |
| XII | The Second Encounter with Force 1 | 109 |
| XIII | Admiral Sir Bruce Fraser closes the Net | 129 |
| XIV | The *Scharnhorst* under Fire | 133 |
| XV | The Destroyer Sub-Divisions of Force 2 attack | 139 |
| XVI | The *Duke of York* attacks for the Second time; Force 2 and Force 1 close in for the Final Battle | 144 |
| XVII | In the Control Position and Port IV 5·9-inch Twin Turret of the *Scharnhorst* | 148 |

7

# CONTENTS

XVIII    *Jamaica, Belfast* and the British Destroyers sink the *Scharnhorst* with Torpedoes    154

XIX    "To All Stations. From the Captain: Abandon Ship!"    157

XX    The Rescue of Survivors by the British Destroyers *Matchless* and *Scorpion*    163

XXI    The Survivors of the *Scharnhorst* Aboard the British Flagship *Duke of York*    171

XXII    Comparison of the Forces participating in the Battle    175

*Bibliography*    177

*Diagrams*    179

*Index*    183

# PLANS

| | | page |
|---|---|---|
| 1. | Sinking of the *Scharnhorst*<br>*Cruiser Operations 0840–1500 hours* | 179 |
| 2. | Sinking of the *Scharnhorst*<br>*Cruiser shadowing and Battleship action 1500–1900 hours* | 180 |
| 3. | Sinking of the *Scharnhorst*<br>*1845–1945 hours* | 181 |

The above plans are reproduced by permission of the Controllers of H.M. Stationery Office from Admiral Sir Bruce Fraser's despatch on the sinking of the *Scharnhorst*, published as a supplement to the *London Gazette* on the 5 August 1947.

# FOREWORD

ON 7 January 1939, the day the *Scharnhorst* was commissioned, her commanding officer, Captain (as he then was) Ciliax, told his officers: "The important thing to remember is this—that the whole life and character of this ship will rest upon the spirit which you officers are able to inculcate in your men." No one could have foreseen how literally true these words were to prove.

In the few months still left before the outbreak of war, the newly assembled crew had to be shaped into a team; under the impact of the manifold operations in which the battleship was subsequently engaged, operations successfully completed in spite of often serious damage, there developed among the men a spontaneous comradeship of rare quality, the true team spirit. Every man of the two thousand who formed the ship's complement was inspired by one conviction, that their ship "sailed under a lucky star".

The author has made full use of all factual material available from both British and German sources and has produced a vivid account of the action off North Cape on 26 December 1943, when the proud ship succumbed to a vastly superior opponent. The exemplary conduct and unflinching devotion to duty of every man on board the *Scharnhorst* were in accordance with the highest traditions of the German Navy.

HELMUTH GIESSLER (Captain, retired)
Navigating Officer and First Officer of
the Battleship *Scharnhorst* from 1939
to 1943

Wilhelmshaven, October 1951

# INTRODUCTION

THE sinking of the *Scharnhorst* is to many people little more than a dim memory; few know what actually happened, for owing to the strict censorship of wartime the details were not published at the time. As, however, the events of that dark Arctic Christmas of 1943 will occupy an important place in the history of naval warfare and as their full significance can now be properly assessed, I have felt justified in telling for the first time the full and authentic story of the sinking of this valiant ship.

In 1940 the names of the German battleships *Scharnhorst* and *Gneisenau* were appearing with some frequency in the British Press. The aircraft-carrier *Glorious* had been sunk and the *Scharnhorst*, whose name had first been in the news in connexion with the sinking of the auxiliary cruiser *Rawalpindi*, had again taken part in the action, as German sources also reported. Unfortunately no survivors could be saved either from the aircraft-carrier or from her two escorting destroyers *Acasta* and *Ardent*. After this incident nothing was heard of the *Scharnhorst* for a while.

Then suddenly, in the spring of 1941, her name was in the news once more. Merchant shipping was being sunk in the Atlantic, and British naval and air forces searched for the German battleship for months on end. But the *Scharnhorst* had disappeared somewhere in the vast expanses of the Atlantic, swallowed up no doubt by the ocean mists or hidden in the heavy swells which ploughed the Atlantic at that time of the year.

Then came the news that the *Scharnhorst* and *Gneisenau* had put into Brest. Cornered at last! The British were confident that the RAF would seek them out and destroy them. Bombs crashed down on the French Atlantic port as the RAF went into action, sending over spotting planes and bombers, while all England waited for the news of the battleships' destruction. But it did not come. The *Scharnhorst* was too well concealed. Trees and shrubs grew on her decks, and camouflage netting intertwined with leaves obstructed the view from the air. True, she did not go completely unscathed at La Pallice, but the hits the RAF were able to score caused no serious damage. The RAF persevered for months, but in vain. The ship lay well hidden, preparing for future action and waiting her chance. Then one day the anchorage lay deserted.

It was on 12 February 1942 that the news broke: "German naval units in the Channel—*Scharnhorst*, *Gneisenau* and *Prinz Eugen*!" The Admiralty was astounded, incredulous.

Everyone wondered how they could possibly have left harbour unnoticed. All the British forces which were available were immediately thrown into action, but these were not formidable, for the naval units most needed lay too far north and it was impossible for them to intervene in time. One or two torpedo-boats and a few out-of-date torpedo-planes and bombers engaged the German units. The coastal artillery fired. In vain. The break-through succeeded. Once more, in company with the destroyers, torpedo-boats, E-boats, mine-sweepers and patrol vessels which covered the break-through in co-operation with the Luftwaffe, this almost legendary ship, the *Scharnhorst*, had slipped from the enemy's grasp.

A little less than two years after this, the BBC broadcast the news that the *Scharnhorst* had been sunk by British naval forces 60 miles NW of North Cape. It happened at a quarter to eight on the evening of December 26th, Boxing Day 1943.

# I

# BIOGRAPHY OF A BATTLESHIP

TO the sailor a ship is a living thing with a life and character of its own, and there are ships that seem sombre and even malevolent, just as there are people whose personalities lack vitality and warmth. The *Scharnhorst* definitely had a soul. Furthermore, she was beautiful, and she sailed with that wonderful, gently swaying motion characteristic of a battleship in a following sea. She seemed always a happy ship, and her spirit pervaded the whole crew, giving rise to a certain fierce pride which was felt by all old *Scharnhorst* men from the Captain down to the humblest rating.

With the grace, elegance and balance of her lines, the *Scharnhorst* was to the sailor's eye a particularly lovely ship. With her sister-ship the *Gneisenau*, she had, right from the early days of the war, taken part in numerous sweeps and sorties and so had become more familiar to the German public than many other ships; indeed in Germany her name was a household word. It had become legendary in the First World War when another *Scharnhorst*, an armoured cruiser, had fought and conquered in the battle of Coronel and later gone down fighting against superior opponents off the Falkland Isles. In the four eventful years of her wartime career the second *Scharnhorst* became a veritable symbol of fortune and success. Seen against the shifting background of the war the *Scharnhorst* did indeed seem to be favoured by fortune to a quite extraordinary degree, an impression confirmed by the war diary of Captain

Giessler, who served in the *Scharnhorst* from the day of her commissioning until shortly before she was sunk.

The outbreak of war found the *Scharnhorst*, after a long period in dock, engaged in trials between Heligoland and the River Jade. She and the *Gneisenau* were the first battleships to be constructed after the lifting of the limitations imposed by the Treaty of Versailles. She was laid down in Wilhelmshaven in 1935, launched on 3 October 1936, and commissioned on 7 January 1939. Captain Ciliax became her first captain. The *Scharnhorst* at this time was not ready for operational duty, still less for front-line action, and in contrast to other newly commissioned ships her complement was drafted from various shore divisions. She was equipped with experimental high-pressure superheated steam boilers. The time available for testing this new machinery and other novel and as yet untried apparatus, as well as for target practice by the ship's guns, was cut short by the outbreak of war. Furthermore the Captain had to go on sick-leave and was replaced by Captain Curt Caesar Hoffmann, who was to take his ship prudently and successfully through her many operations right up to 1942.

It was evident from the offensive measures taken by the German Navy immediately following the outbreak of war, that the much maligned "big" ships, the "chained watch-dogs" of the First World War, were not again to lie idly in their bases but were to come out and attack British merchant shipping. Anti-aircraft action against British planes in early engagements of the war was not the only trial by fire which the new, powerful, beautifully built ships had to undergo. Unfortunately—from the German point of view—as the heavier guns had not yet been re-introduced, their main armament consisted only of three 11-inch triple turrets.

At the beginning of September 1939, after passing through the Kaiser-Wilhelm Canal—the first 26,000-ton battleship to do so, work on deepening the canal having only just been completed—the *Scharnhorst* reached Kiel. Here a new secret apparatus, known at the time as *Dete* or E.M.2, was mounted; it was the Radar equipment which, after being perfected by the British, was to play such an important role in the ultimate sinking of the *Scharnhorst*.

At midday on 21 November 1939 the two battleships, which had been moved to Wilhelmshaven at the beginning of November, sailed down the River Jade. The Commander-in-Chief, Vice-Admiral Marschall, flew his flag in the *Gneisenau*. Aboard the *Scharnhorst* Captain Hoffmann announced the object of the operation over the loudspeaker system; it was to be a sweep against the patrol forces operating between Iceland and the Faroes. Officers and men were taken by surprise; no vessel of the high-seas fleet had ever ventured so far during the First World War.

"We are like rats coming out of their holes," a Sub-Lieutenant remarked happily. "And we'll show them we can bite."

The Force first shaped course to the northward, proceeding behind the so-called West Wall, the mine-belt which protected the North Friesian islands from attack. Orders were given for war watches to be posted. Destroyers formed a screen against hostile submarines. The great Radar grid revolved in ghostly fashion on the foretop, but picked up nothing. On the 22nd at 2 a. n., the mine-belt was crossed and the destroyers were dismissed. The Force now proceeded on its own without lights through the pitch-dark night at roughly twenty-seven knots. Around noon the battleships passed through the narrowest stretch of water between the Shetland Isles and the Norwegian coast. Luftwaffe cover extended thus far.

The weather soon began to deteriorate. A south-west

B

wind, force 7/8, and a long and high ground-swell made the ships roll badly, bringing on the first cases of sea-sickness. The guns suffered some small structural damage from the vast masses of water which were breaking on board. All this was new, unfamiliar experience, but it helped to establish a more intimate contact between ship and crew. Altering course to the north-west the Force proceeded. During the night of November 22nd–23rd it passed the Faroes at a distance of thirty sea miles and made for Iceland. Though on the following day visibility was excellent, nothing was sighted. The wireless signals which were picked up were similarly negative though the ships were then passing in broad formation through the actual home waters of the British Home Fleet. At 1607 hours a report from the foretop alerted the bridge: "Starboard beam, a big steamer! Still very distant. Details not yet visible."

"Might be a merchant ship," suggested Captain Hoffmann, "or possibly an auxiliary cruiser doing escort duty. I'll have a look myself."

The Captain climbed to the foretop. After a while his voice came through the foretop telephone: "She's altering course repeatedly and is not flying any flag."

Orders were given to close with the steamer. After half an hour the Captain gave the alarm and returned to the bridge. He informed the Admiral on board the *Gneisenau* of his observations. When the steamer did not obey the order to heave-to the *Scharnhorst* opened fire and the first shells were soon bursting on the target. The steamer pluckily returned the fire but without success, then she put up a smoke screen and tried to escape. But she was already in flames when the *Gneisenau*, speeding up from the southward, also opened fire. Blazing like a torch in the swiftly gathering darkness, the battered ship lay helpless with her engines stopped. Morse signals flickered out from the pall of smoke and fumes. It was reported from the signal bridge of the *Scharnhorst* that the vessel was signalling for help.

Boats were drifting about. The *Scharnhorst* reduced her speed and allowed the boats to come alongside so that survivors could be picked up. As yet another boat drew alongside a signal was received from the *Gneisenau*: "Break off rescue operations at once. Follow!" The Captain looked questioningly at the First Officer who had appeared on the bridge to report on the rescue operations; then word came through from one of the look-out posts: "Shadow dead astern."

Captain Hoffmann rushed to one end of the bridge:

"Let go the painter! All engines full speed ahead!"

The battleships made off eastwards at high speed. The British cruiser *Newcastle*, coming up from astern, tried to engage them but fell behind. She rescued the remaining survivors of the 16,000-ton auxiliary cruiser P. & O. Liner *Rawalpindi*, whose gallant commander, Captain E. C. Kennedy, had so heroically joined battle against such hopeless odds. The British Home Fleet now tried to intercept the two German battleships on the home stretch but without success. The meteorologists aboard the *Scharnhorst* predicted poor visibility and a southerly gale below the Norwegian coast. For two whole days the ships stood by, waiting to the northward. Then suddenly the barograph dropped abruptly and the ships headed south. During the night of November 25th–26th, in a rising gale, they were able to head for Cape Stadlandet in Norway at 27 knots. The return to base was accomplished in ferocious weather. Spray flew to the foretop, the decks were awash, and the heavy ships were practically submerged. For twenty-four hours they had to be commanded from the conning-tower because the bridges were completely under water. A single trawler was again sighted at a point about on a level with Bergen, rolling heavily athwart the ships' course. The wind turned more and more towards the south, and soon rough seas were flooding the forward turrets. Below the coast of Jutland German destroyers linked up with them and on November 27th the ships lay once more at anchor in the River Jade.

The first operation had been successfully completed. The battleships had proved their worth. With their high speed and extensive range—the bunkers held 6,000 tons of oil—they were excellently suited to deliver surprise attacks on British merchant shipping. But, and even more important, this successful operation in storm conditions had had the effect of welding the crew firmly together; they had found their sea-legs, they had got to know their ship and had seen what she was capable of. In the fire of the guns, the howl of the gale and the roar of the sea the foundations of that unique and steadfast comradeship which was later to manifest itself, had been laid.

In January 1940 there were further exercises in the Baltic. It was an exceptional winter and the freeze-up was of great severity. The ships, moored to their buoys in Kiel, became frozen-in and the liberty men went ashore on foot, a strange sight indeed! In March one of the patrol vessels broke up the ice and the battleships were ordered back to the North Sea for fresh assignments. For the moment this meant more waiting, just as the troops behind the Siegfried Line were condemned to wait during the "phony war" period. The unchanging spectacle of seagulls drifting seaward on ice floes with the outgoing tide in the morning and returning up-river on the afternoon tide, became almost unendurable. A brief and uneventful sortie to Stavanger relieved the monotony a little. The weather turned gradually warmer. British air-raids increased and soon the A.A. guns were kept busy even during the hours of daylight.

For a short spell the *Scharnhorst* put into port. Something was in the air. No one knew anything definite but the whole ship was soon in a fever of excitement and everyone was convinced that an important operation was pending. The operation order was in fact already locked up in the secret compartment of the Navigating Officer's desk. The document was headed "Exercise Weser", the code name for the occupation of Norway and Denmark. This bold enterprise had been entrusted to the Navy, and it could be successfully carried out only if absolute secrecy was maintained. On April 6th, when the *Scharnhorst* was lying once more in the roadstead, the Commander-in-Chief came on board and apprised the ship's company of the impending operation. The men were jubilant, and proud of the trust placed in them by the Supreme Command.

During the night of April 6th–7th the Force put to sea. It consisted again of the two battleships *Scharnhorst* and *Gneisenau*, joined before Wangerooge by the heavy cruiser *Admiral Hipper* with four escorting destroyers and a flotilla of ten destroyers which, as the so-called Narvik Group, was later to win fame off the North Norwegian coast. Just as they were assembling, a low-flying aircraft came swooping down towards them; it was an anxious moment, but fire from the *Scharnhorst's* anti-aircraft guns forced it to turn away and it disappeared before it had identified the other ships in the darkness. The vessels proceeded northward at high speed. From dawn onwards ship-borne aircraft provided fighter protection while destroyers formed an anti-submarine screen for the heavy units. On the afternoon of April 7th off the Skagerrak the look-outs on all ships gave the alarm:

"Several formations of enemy aircraft!"

The anti-aircraft guns of every ship fired in concert at the reconnaissance aircraft sweeping over them. On every bridge the same anxious questions were discussed.

Was the object of the operation known? What were the British up to? In spite of doubts and fears the ships held their course. The weather was still good. The exceptionally dark night of the 7th–8th wrapped the ships in its all-concealing mantle. As they passed the narrowest part of the sea between the Shetlands and Norway, the look-outs stared into the impenetrable blackness with redoubled concentration. Nothing was sighted. On the morning of the 8th the weather deteriorated rapidly. A rough sea sprang up, the wind veered and freshened appreciably. Soon it was blowing force 7 from the southwest. The destroyers laboured heavily as ever more frequently they transmitted the signal:

"Shadowed by several formations of enemy aircraft!"

Speed was reduced so that the destroyers could keep station. A few destroyers standing further below the Norwegian coast joined battle with British destroyers on the same morning. The *Admiral Hipper* received orders to turn round and to close one of the German destroyers *Bernd v. Arnim*. Aboard the *Scharnhorst* the Captain discussed the situation with his Navigating Officer:

"I don't understand it. What are the British destroyers doing at sea? No other British forces have been reported, have they?"

Korvettenkapitän Giessler shook his head:

"No, Herr Kapitän, not yet. . . ."

"Important wireless message, sir," broke in the Second W/T Officer. "The British have just given a mine-warning for an extensive area below the Norwegian coast. Obviously they have laid new mine-fields there."

Captain Hoffmann scrutinized the message: "What can it mean? Have they got the same idea as we have? Are they screening their own occupation of Norway against our naval forces? Come with me, Giessler, let's look at the charts."

As they disappeared into the chart-house the other officers on the bridge discussed this new development. Meanwhile the Force proceeded on its course. Then the *Admiral Hipper* with her four escorting destroyers left the Narvik Group and headed to the entrance to Trondhjem Fjord. When the battleships reached the mouth of West Fjord in pitch darkness at 2100 hours they detached the ten destroyers of the Narvik Group (i.e. the flotilla destined for the occupation of Narvik) according to plan. The *Scharnhorst* and *Gneisenau* remained near the Lofoten Islands during the night to cover the destroyer flotilla from the rear. A severe storm was now raging. The battleships laboured heavily, steaming at a reduced speed to save fuel. It was not until the early hours of the 8th that the weather moderated to intermittent snow-squalls; visibility even became excellent at times. In the early morning hours the Navigating Officer on board the *Scharnhorst* was able to use the sextant. He had been unable to fix the ship's position by astronomical sights for some time and he intended now to make another attempt. He lifted the instrument and —instead of the expected star—got the red flashes of heavy guns in the mirror!

"Alarm!"

Bells screamed, the watches below rushed to action stations; orders from the bridge, signals from the flag-ship and first firing instructions came through in quick succession, and in a few minutes the barrels of the 11-inch guns were thundering at the vessel which hove into sight faintly silhouetted against the dark western sky. In dense swirling snow the two battleships with-drew northward at top speed. The running encounter lasted from 0510 to 0659 hours with the *Scharnhorst* and *Gneisenau* firing from the stern. Heavy 15-inch shells exploded close to the *Scharnhorst* as her Captain by repeatedly changing course managed to out-manœuvre each new salvo.

"The enemy's flying an Admiral's flag," reported the Gunnery Commander. Then, "It's the *Renown*!"

But the British vessel could not keep pace with the high speed of the Germans; soon she dropped astern and was ultimately lost to sight in the whirling snow. The *Scharnhorst* with her customary good luck had suffered no damage. Her engines had developed some minor troubles but having regard to their experimental design and the severe strain put upon them this was no more than might have been expected, and they were quickly put right. The Force sailed northward for a few hours and then altered course to westward almost reaching the longitude of the lonely rock-island of Jan Mayen. Meanwhile on board wireless messages were coming in all the time about the occupation of Norway and Denmark. Reports that the British Fleet was at sea alternated with news of ferocious air battles and points of resistance on land. The battleships could not themselves transmit without betraying their position, and the High Command at home still knew nothing of the encounter. On the 10th therefore the *Scharnhorst* catapulted an aircraft which was to take a wireless message from the Commander-in-Chief to Trondhjem for transmission from there. The plane had to start from the extreme limit of its range. With a full tank the *Arado 196* took off, piloted by First Lieutenant Schreck with First Lieutenant Schrewe as observer. They had only a map of Trondhjem Fjord on board and apart from that no maritime charts at all. Would they make Trondhjem and reach the *Admiral Hipper*? There were hours of anxious suspense until at last the *Admiral Hipper* reported that the aircraft had landed. It was a brilliant feat on the part of the *Arado* crew. The men in the

*Scharnhorst* learned later how amazed the commander of the heavy cruiser had been when the observer appeared on deck.

"What next?" Captain Heye had said. "I've only just heard from British reports that the *Scharnhorst* and *Gneisenau* have been sunk!"

It had been planned that the battleships should pick up the destroyer flotilla of the Narvik Group on their return journey, but all ten destroyers were lost. The fuel position now forced the battleships to return to base. Wireless reports from Germany had established that, together with many other British ships, the aircraft-carrier *Furious* was at sea and had almost certainly been instructed to bring aircraft into action against the German battleships. Hence the Commander-in-Chief worked round further westward in order then, in the darkness of night, and standing only 60 miles off the Shetland Isles, to turn south. Once more a bad weather front came to the aid of the fortunate ships. Unsighted by the enemy they arrived at noon at the agreed rendezvous to pick up the *Admiral Hipper* and their destroyer screen. After the vessels had taken up station their ship-borne aircraft took off to patrol against enemy submarines. Later a British reconnaissance plane spotted the ships and several waves of bombers later came over, but in the poor visibility they did not find them.

On April 12th the convoy anchored at Wilhelmshaven. An important operation had been successfully accomplished; the men had learned much in the hard school of war and had become seasoned sailors. Their confidence in themselves, their officers and their ship was now unshakeable.

Six weeks of docking were needed to overhaul various parts of the machinery and guns. Then both battleships and their escorting destroyers were once again ready for action. Meanwhile the operational position had changed fundamentally and in Germany's favour. The campaign in France was at an end. Bases further to the west and in Norway were now available and a route through the Skagerrak and Danish waters was open as an alternative to that through the North Sea which was exposed to submarine and air attack. But the battle for Narvik was still on and the outcome remained uncertain. It fell to the *Scharnhorst*, *Gneisenau*, *Admiral Hipper* and a comparatively small number of destroyers to force a decision.

On 4 June 1940 the Force, commanded once more by Vice-Admiral Marschall, sailed from Kiel. It passed the German mine-barrier near Skagen and proceeded northward. There was some uncertainty as to the current disposition of British naval forces; the possible presence of battleships in the region of Narvik as well as sorties from Scapa Flow had also to be reckoned with. Now and again submarine periscopes were sighted, but the submarines were not given the chance to attack. The Luftwaffe, operating now from Trondhjem, had a far wider range for reconnaissance. Brilliant summer weather prevailed, interrupted only by isolated showers which temporarily reduced visibility, and during these periods the Radar apparatus could be relied upon to prevent unpleasant surprises. The destroyers, fuelled by the battleships, sailed this time with the main force. For the first time too a supply ship participated, the *Dithmarschen*, from which the *Admiral Hipper* could refuel. At this season there were in these latitudes practically twenty-four hours of daylight, so that the fuelling operations could be continued well into the night.

As in peacetime the Commander-in-Chief ordered the captains to a conference aboard the flagship. Air reconnaissance over Harstad and Narvik had been called off owing to weather conditions over the coastline, and the Admiral had therefore no information as to the British naval forces operating there. However, not far off several small convoys steering a south-westerly course had been spotted. On the morning of June 8th the three heavy ships with their four destroyers deployed in a broad reconnaissance sweep and approached the convoys. Ship-borne aircraft were catapulted and likewise flew reconnaissance. Soon one of the German destroyers made out a tanker and duly sent it to the bottom. Further vessels were sighted by the ships or reported by aircraft, and these too were sunk by the *Admiral Hipper* and the destroyers. It so happened that a hospital ship which, as later came to light, had a number of German prisoners from Narvik on board, was allowed to go without being searched. At midday the *Admiral Hipper* and the destroyers were ordered to Trondhjem to replenish supplies. The *Scharnhorst* and *Gneisenau*, however, continued operations in the sea area off northern Norway. In view of the lack of air reconnaissance the Commander-in-Chief decided not to carry out the order to make for Harstad but to operate instead against the convoys. He pushed ahead with the Battle Group at a speed of 18 knots into the sea area between Harstad and Tromsoe. At 1645 hours on June 8th a report came through from the *Scharnhorst's* foretop that a distant cloud of smoke had been briefly visible.

Asked for a more detailed description by the Captain, the lookout, Midshipman Goss, explained: "It was a short blast of smoke, like a blubber when there's a bit of trouble with the boilers. Bearings are precisely laid."

"Alarm!" commanded Captain Hoffmann. At the same time he ordered the ship to be turned at top speed into the direction indicated and reported to the Admiral. The *Gneisenau* joined in the manœuvre. The range closed rapidly and soon a mast, then a stocky funnel and then the superstructure hove in sight above the horizon. At 27 miles the first range was taken and simultaneously the Gunnery Commander reported:

"To the Captain—Ship is unmistakably an aircraft-carrier, probably the *Glorious* with two escorting destroyers!"

At 28,000 yards the heavy guns opened up, while shortly afterwards the secondary armament took the destroyers under fire. The Captain, standing with the Navigating Officer at the periscope of the control position, looked up. "Poor devil!" he said. "Our luck's in again. Two battleships against one aircraft-carrier!"

In the target area the first covering salvo straddled the flight deck, which was packed tight with aircraft. Angry flashes flared into dazzling sheets of red flame, and an enormous pall of smoke enveloped the luckless carrier.

"The destroyers put up a magnificent fight," the Navigating Officer commented later. "They used the same tactics as the British cruisers had adopted against the *Graf Spee* in the River Plate[1]: one of them laid down a smoke-screen while the other went in to attack. But it didn't help them much."

The destroyers were the *Ardent* and *Acasta*, trying in vain to conceal their carrier *Glorious* and at the same time to take the offensive against the battleships. Direct hits battered the superstructure of the brave little ships; in spite of their hopeless situation they closed in again and again to fire their torpedoes. Meanwhile the crippled *Glorious* lay motionless beneath a massive cloud of smoke from which the flashes of explosions broke continuously while white pillars of water marked shell splashes in the sea. Both battleships kept close observation on the torpedoes fired by the destroyers and manœuvred out of the way of several

[1] It should be noted that this account of the River Plate action is based on German sources. British reports indicate that it was the *Graf Spee* which laid down a smoke-screen.

which were either sighted or located by hydrophone. The battle had already been on for nearly two hours, and still the British destroyers were putting up a heroic but desperate stand. By forcing the German battleships to take evasive action they were able to embarrass their artillery. At 1839 a report reached the *Scharnhorst's* bridge: "Heavy detonation in stern!"

The individual reports came in promptly as if on a peacetime exercise: " 'C' turret evacuated. Magazine 'C' turret flooded."

The *Scharnhorst* lost speed. A quickly increasing list to starboard became noticeable. Then the engine-room reported:

"One engine still working. No definite reports have yet been received from the other two. Probably hit by torpedo."

Speed fell to 20 knots. One of the destroyers had been sunk but the other was still firing and even scored a hit on one barrel of B turret. The *Scharnhorst* again closed the *Gneisenau*. At about 1900 hours, the second destroyer too was sunk.

"Lull in action: attend to casualties."

The men worked feverishly while damage control parties strove to stem the inrush of water, for no less than 2,500 tons had been shipped. In the engine-room Chief Engineer Liebhardt was trying to assess the damage to the centre and starboard engines. The port engine was still functioning, but one turret was out of action, and in it forty men had lost their lives. At 20 knots the Force made for Trondhjem which was reached in the afternoon of June 6th. The repair ship was lying there with its crew of specialist artificers who at once went to work to put the *Scharnhorst* back into commission. After ten days of uninterrupted labour the centre engine was working again. This was a magnificent achievement on the part of the Chief Engineer and his men, who with the support of the repair ship *Huaskaran*, had had to work under repeated attack from carrier-borne enemy aircraft. One bomb had actually landed on the upper deck, but had failed to explode. The ship's own aircraft were kept busy keeping British submarines out of Trondhjem Fjord. On June 20th the *Scharnhorst* had two engines functioning perfectly and was ready for her return journey. The starboard propeller had to be lashed fast as it was feared that the shaft had been cracked by the torpedo.

At 24 knots she left port, hugging as far as possible the coast behind the rocky islets of the Schären. In fine weather, with very good visibility and a strong wind—which was an embarrassment to the two escorting torpedo-boats—and protected by her own fighter aircraft, the *Scharnhorst* proceeded south, passing at midday on the 21st to seaward of the Schären Isles. A British reconnaissance plane again discovered the Force, its screen having now been reinforced by another two destroyers and two torpedo-boats. Could this reconnaissance plane call bombers to the scene? The answer was not long in coming. For nearly two hours on end wave after wave appeared as the RAF attacked the Force with bombs and torpedoes off the Isle of Utsire. But the dense hail of A.A. shells repelled all attacks. Many of the bombers, hit by A.A. fire or shot down by fighters, crashed into the sea leaving long trails of smoke behind them. In the *Scharnhorst* alone the expenditure of ammunition during this defence action ran to 900 rounds of 4·1 inch, 1,200 rounds of 37 mm. and 2,400 rounds of 20 mm. shells! At 1815 hours the Captain received a wireless message from Group West:

"Put into Stavanger!"

Captain Hoffmann looked at the signal in amazement. "It's incomprehensible," he said. "What's the use of that narrow anchorage to us? Still, they must have their reasons for ordering us there ..."

A few hours later the ships anchored in the limited space of Stavanger harbour. Group West had indeed had valid reasons for their order as now emerged: the Supreme Naval Command had learned through monitoring the British W/T traffic that practically the whole British Home Fleet was at sea with the object of catching the *Scharnhorst*. But within one hour of the situation becoming known, the *Scharnhorst* was already on her way to the fjord. It was a lucky escape. Next morning, air reconnaissance was able to report that the British fleet, consisting of at least four battleships, four cruisers and several destroyers, was on its way back to Scapa Flow. Unnoticed by the enemy the *Scharnhorst* and her escort again put to sea and slipped into Kiel where repairs were immediately put in hand.

This operation, in which the crew had sustained its first losses, strengthened in all the men the conviction that the ship's company, officers and ratings alike, formed a well-knit whole which would withstand all adversity. The victorious battle, the perilous return with the disabled ship, as well as the successful repulsion of many air attacks, could not but deepen their belief that the *Scharnhorst* bore a charmed life.

Dockyard refitting of the two battleships lasted for practically six months, and it was not until the autumn that they lay ready for action in their new base at Gotenhaven. Since newly established bases had become available on the west coast of France the High Command was paying increased attention to operations in the Atlantic. So, at the end of 1940 both battleships, commanded by their new Commander-in-Chief, Admiral Lütjens, sailed from Kiel. In the northern North Sea a heavy gale caused considerable damage to the *Gneisenau* and the whole Force had to return home.

But on 22 January 1941 both battleships were able to leave harbour again. The order which Admiral Lütjens carried with him was, for a German battleship, without precedent: To wage war on merchant shipping in the northern Atlantic. It was understood that in this type of warfare, contact with heavy British fighting units was, if possible, to be avoided.

The operation had been carefully planned and prepared. A number of tankers were standing by in the Atlantic from which oil, ammunition and stores could be replenished. Other German warships were operating in the Atlantic at the same time: the pocket-battleship *Admiral Scheer*, the heavy cruiser *Admiral Hipper*, a number of auxiliary cruisers and U-boats. It was a daring undertaking for a fleet which had been under strength at the outbreak of war and had not yet been fully built up.

In the dark night of the new moon the Force made for the narrows south of Iceland, and in the small hours of January 28th, in the so-called "Rose Garden", they ran into a British cruiser line. Under cover of darkness the Force hauled round and retreated to the northward without having been spotted. A ship-borne aircraft informed Group North of what was intended next: to refuel from the tanker *Adria* standing by east of Jan Mayen and to break through to the Atlantic north of Iceland along the edge of the pack-ice. Both operations succeeded. On February 4th the Commander-in-Chief was able to transmit the signal to his Force: "For the first time in history German battleships have succeeded in breaking through to the Atlantic. Now—go to it!"

After further refuelling from a tanker south of Greenland they began to search for convoys. At last, on February 8th, masts were sighted. The *Scharnhorst*, however, soon realized that the convoy sighted was covered by a battleship, the *Ramillies*, and in accordance with her instructions, did not attack. Further search, which was continued along the northern convoy route, was hampered by severe gales and Admiral Lütjens decided to proceed to the south where the convoy route had evidently been shifted. It was getting warmer and the men were glad after their long sojourn in colder regions to change from fur and woollen clothing into lighter wear. But the search again was abortive, even on the much-frequented route between Freetown and England. Only a solitary Greek steamer was sunk. Fuelling took place about every eight days. The weather remained settled with consistently good visibility. Ship-borne aircraft took off continuously for reconnaissance flights, but there was still nothing to be seen. Not until March 7th was another convoy sighted. U-boats were now co-operating for the first time and the battleships effectively assisted them in their attack on the convoy which again was covered by a battleship, this time the *Malaya*. The *Scharnhorst* and *Gneisenau* were able to claim an indirect success when the U-boats sniped 43,000 tons of shipping from the convoy in two nights. After this, operations were shifted back northward to the route between North America and Great Britain. Two escorting tankers helped to extend the reconnaissance area. Successes against solitary ships— targets authorized by the Commander-in-Chief—accumulated; one ship after another went to the bottom. In less than two days, sixteen vessels, representing a total of 75,000 tons, fell victim to the battleships. Success had come at last after the long wearying search. With surprising speed the gun crews developed a technique for sinking the ships with shots accurately placed on the waterline. The ground swell and rough sea often impeded the picking up of survivors from their lifeboats. Everything had to be done quickly as there was always the possibility that British naval forces would suddenly appear on the scene, and on March 16th this happened. The *Scharnhorst* had just sunk a ship when, in the falling dusk, a wireless message came in from one of her own tankers.

"Enemy battleship sighted!"

The *Gneisenau*, which was standing close to the tanker, was even challenged. But the half-light and the now famous rain-storm which always seemed to inter-vene obligingly at such moments, allowed the battle-ships to escape.

As there was small prospect of any further success on this route the operation was called off, and on 22 March 1941, exactly two months after sailing from Kiel, the two ships entered the new Atlantic base at Brest. Never before had German battleships carried out an operation of such long duration. Though it was true that no convoys had been sunk, the disturbance to British merchant shipping and the disorganization of Royal Naval dispositions were considerable and in them-selves eminently worthwhile from the German point of view. Furthermore, it was hoped that the experience which had been gained in the undertaking could be put to good account in subsequent operations which were to be carried out in company with the recently completed battleship *Bismarck*. The conduct of the men remained beyond praise, particularly that of the engine-room personnel who had never failed to come up to the high standard of performance required of them in spite of frequent technical trouble. Once more fortune had smiled on the sister ships.

The French Naval dockyard at Brest, which had been taken over by the Wilhelmshaven dockyard, at once commenced the necessary work of refitting. The RAF, however, were soon on the scene, and heavier and heavier attacks were launched on the battleships. In one of these raids, which also destroyed large areas of the town, the *Gneisenau* was hit and as a result the repair period was prolonged. The *Scharnhorst*, the "lucky ship", remained undamaged and was fully ready for action again by July 1941. In the meantime the British had succeeded in cornering and sinking the *Bismarck* after her break-through to the Atlantic. The *Prinz Eugen*, which had been accompanying the battleship, escaped and also sought refuge in Brest. The *Scharnhorst* was now transferred to La Pallice, a port to the south of Brest. She was obliged to leave harbour for trials of her new superheater and other machine components and in spite of the heaviest camouflage was spotted by the British. In the midday hours of July 24th under a cloudless sky, the *Scharnhorst* was attacked by a high-flying formation. Flak and fighter protection could not ward off the attack. A row of five bombs hit the ship from stem to stern. Three heavy armour-piercing bombs penetrated the upper deck, but failed to explode. The two smaller bombs exploded in the battery deck but caused only negligible damage. Flooding caused by the three heavy bombs was however quite considerable. The ship took in 3,000 tons of water, but the list caused could be compensated and the cable defects were promptly repaired. But even now good luck had not deserted the *Scharnhorst*, for there were, miraculously, no casualties. She returned to Brest at 27 knots and in spite of recurrent air-raids and frequent shifts of berth the dock repairs to the two battleships were almost completed by the turn of the year 1941–2.

Meanwhile the superiority of British and American forces in the Atlantic had become established and to risk the two battleships in the North Atlantic was now out of the question. The only opportunity for mercantile warfare that remained was against the Arctic convoys sailing north of Norway to Murmansk. But how were the three big ships to be brought safely from Brest into their home waters? After long deliberation the High Command decided to attempt a break-through up the English Channel. This without doubt was the most dangerous course of action, but if absolute secrecy could be maintained and the enemy were taken completely by surprise, it promised the greatest chance of success.

Detailed planning began at once. Vice-Admiral Ciliax took over the command and was responsible for the initial stages of preparation. Even before the refitting of the ships had been completed, mine-sweeping flotillas were sent out to clear a safe passage. Continuous fighter protection by the Luftwaffe was arranged and provided for. Two hundred and fifty aircraft were made available to serve as a continuous air umbrella and enormous fuel reserves were held ready at appropriate places; new airfields were laid out and the liaison between ships and fighter cover was tried out. The closely woven net of powerful Radar installations along the English Channel coast had to be paralysed by jamming stations, which again entailed much detailed planning and preparation. Finally, all seaworthy destroyers and torpedo-boats had to be concentrated in Brest and this meant that they would have to be transferred westward through the Channel. Even this somewhat conspicuous move apparently remained unnoticed by the British, or at any rate did not arouse their suspicions. Rumours about an imminent Atlantic operation were deliberately spread. The Luftwaffe Wing Commander invited admirals and captains to a grand hunting party, the impressive invitation cards being sent by post. Entertainments for the crews were organized in and outside Brest; in short, every possible trick of camouflage was assiduously put into practice. The actual sailing date depended on the concurrence of certain optimum weather conditions: low cloud and haze in the Channel, a new moon and a strong tidal current running with the ships. At last the meteorologist was able to predict the desired conditions. The mine-sweeping divisions reported the route clear, the destroyers were assembled intact in Brest and the fighter umbrella stood ready on call.

For the evening of 11 February 1942 a night encounter exercise was arranged on board the *Scharnhorst*. This helped to camouflage the raising of steam which would of course be necessary for such an exercise. Steam-up was ordered for 2030 hours and most of the hawsers had been cast off, when the routine enemy reconnaissance aircraft appeared over the port and illuminated the area with flares. Port and ships had to be quickly concealed in smoke and the Force left harbour two hours behind schedule, the Admiral sailing in the *Scharnhorst*. However, the assembling outside the net barrage was accomplished in shorter time than had been anticipated, and one hour was quickly made up. Still only a few officers knew what was actually afoot. In the *Scharnhorst*, the Officer of the Watch, slightly troubled at the absence of explicit orders, asked the Navigating Officer for the course:

"Question: new course, Sir?"

Kapitän Giessler smiled. "Next course twenty degrees. Tomorrow you'll be kissing your mother good night in Wilhelmshaven!"

The excitement on the bridge, soon to be shared by the whole ship, was indescribable.

Protected by a screen of destroyers, and sailing at 27 knots, the Force made its way eastwards. At 0700 hours Cherbourg was passed and at dawn the fleet fighters and light bombers took over the air cover. During the night a flotilla of mine-sweepers had discovered a newly laid mine-field around the mouth of the Seine, but the Force was eased through it at a reduced speed behind the sweepers, after the Admiral had given the signal "Boom gap marked!" And then, through the mist which, according to forecast, lay over the Channel, the shimmering white cliffs of Dover came into view. Far off a single British aircraft appeared; direction shots marked it as a target for the Force's own fighters, and soon it was sent crashing into the Channel in flames. At noon—strictly according to time-table—the narrowest part of the Channel between Dover and Cap Gris Nez was left behind. There was still no sign of any British counter-measures. Why were the enemy's heavy shore batteries still silent? Quietness reigned. And then at last there came a flash out of the haze—a single battery had opened fire, but its shots fell harmlessly into the grey-green waters of the Channel far to port. E-boats promptly laid down a smoke-screen. In the *Scharnhorst* the astro-navigator remarked to the Navigating Officer:

"It's coming off like a navigation practice cruise."

As the route wound through the many sand bars below the Thames estuary, British defences at last became active. One squadron of Swordfish torpedo-planes and another of Beaufighters attacked the Force but all were shot down. Later, waves of bombers followed, but the naval aircraft and the ships' continuously firing A.A. guns made accurate aiming impossible. Fine drizzle set in and visibility deteriorated. The *Scharnhorst* had frequently to change course to avoid bombs, while mine-sweepers were still at work. A marker boat was just being passed when, at around 1530 hours, a heavy blow shook the whole ship and lifted her out of the water. The engines stopped, the electrical current failed and the ship was plunged into sudden darkness. Quietly and efficiently the reports came in from the various stations. The engine-room reported a small amount of flooding and declared that the engines would have to be stopped for a while.

The Admiral promptly ordered a destroyer to stand

by and transferred to her. Whatever happened he must carry on with the command of the squadron.

While the *Gneisenau* and *Prinz Eugen* continued on their course screened by their escort vessels, the *Scharnhorst* was obliged to remain immobile for half an hour. But once more the ship was favoured by fortune, for during the whole of this time not one enemy aircraft was sighted. At last came the word of deliverance:

"Port engine running."

The *Scharnhorst* gathered way. Soon all three engines were working again and at 1604 hours the ship was forging ahead once more at 27 knots. She was protected by several torpedo-boats. The other ships were far ahead. It was learned in the *Scharnhorst* from wireless signals that the Force had had an encounter with an enemy cruiser and destroyers. Meanwhile attacks by the six hundred bombers which the British had now thrown into the action, were going on. One torpedo-boat received a direct hit and, with another boat to escort it, had to be detached to make for the Hook of Holland. The clouds hung lower and the way in which the naval craft protected the ship in spite of swiftly deteriorating visibility, was wholly admirable. Air attack followed air attack in relentless sequence until darkness fell, but without success. The sea lane along the Dutch coast, known as Easy Street, was not so easy as all that; there were sandbanks to starboard and to port it was alive with mines. To add to the difficulties, the *Scharnhorst's* echo-sounder and D/F (direction-finder) set had been jolted out of action by the mine explosion. Through the haze ahead loomed two destroyers with a cutter between them lying athwart the ship's course.

"The Admiral's in the cutter!" exclaimed the navigating boatswain.

Admiral Ciliax had had to leave his first destroyer owing to engine damage and had transferred to yet another vessel. The *Scharnhorst* had to reduce speed so as not to capsize the cutter in her stern wash. The Admiral told later what a great moment it had been for him when the *Scharnhorst* with her mighty bow-wave suddenly hove in sight out of the haze. He had been thinking that she might have had to seek refuge in some Dutch emergency harbour. The night closed in, dark and misty. The *Scharnhorst* was passing the marker boat lying off Terschelling dead on time when at 2234 hours another detonation shook the ship. Fortunately once more only a small amount of water was shipped and the engines too were in working order again soon after the explosion. At slow speed she was steered towards the rendezvous point with the anti-boom ship which was to guide her to Wilhelmshaven. The other ships had already reached the Elbe when, on 13 February 1942, the *Scharnhorst* entered Wilhelmshaven. The impossible had been achieved. Within range of the heavy shore batteries on the English coast the German Force, covered by its screen of escorting vessels and the Luftwaffe, had slipped through almost unmolested under the very nose of the British defences. "Britain's greatest blunder" was the comment of one newspaper, while *The Times* admitted ruefully that not since the seventeenth century had the British Fleet suffered such humiliation in its home waters.

And what of the men of the *Scharnhorst*, the crew who under exceptionally trying conditions had once more proved themselves? "Nothing can happen to us," they were saying. "Ours is a lucky ship."

The *Scharnhorst* docked for a short time at Wilhelmshaven so that the extent of the underwater damage could be properly assessed. Then she sailed on to Kiel for repairs. Now the *Scharnhorst* and *Gneisenau* lay side by side in the dockyard, while the RAF threw in everything they had to put these dangerous opponents out of action. The *Gneisenau* received a decisive hit which blew up the ammunition of the forward turret and tore away almost the entire bow. Thus the sister ship was put out of commission while the *Scharnhorst* remained miraculously intact.

On 1 April 1942, Captain Hoffmann, who had commanded the ship for three years and had now been promoted Rear-Admiral and decorated with the Knight's Cross, handed over the command to Captain Hüffmeier. In October of the same year the ship was again ready for sea, and in January 1943 she was reported from Gotenhaven fit for front-line service. The long-standing plan to move her to Norway was carried out in March 1943. Without the staff of a flag officer on board and escorted only by two destroyers she sailed to West Fjord. There the battle group stationed in northern Norway assembled: *Tirpitz*, *Admiral Scheer*, *Scharnhorst*, and a handful of cruisers and destroyers. Shortly afterwards the *Tirpitz* and *Scharnhorst* shifted berth to the Alta and Lang Fjords in the extreme north, close to the route taken by the Arctic convoys to Russia. During the summer of 1943 the *Tirpitz* and *Scharnhorst* undertook an offensive sweep to Spitzbergen, where the coalmines were flooded and other important installations destroyed. For the moment, however, no attack upon the convoys was launched as the essential conditions—adequate air reconnaissance and favourable weather—were lacking.

The *Scharnhorst* had, by the summer of 1943, been hit by mine, bomb, torpedo and shell during her many operations; but throughout it all she had remained the successful, the "lucky" ship. Her crew had been welded by selfless comradeship, loyalty and love of their ship into a close, battle-hardened community, and her luck held until that fateful day in December 1943 which marked her end.

# II

# THE NAVAL AND MILITARY SITUATION
# IN 1943

IT is difficult accurately to reconstruct the last operation of the *Scharnhorst*, at any rate from German
sources, for of the crew of just on 1,900 only 36 were
saved, and of these survivors not one was of commissioned rank. The author has therefore drawn upon both
German and British eye-witness accounts and memo-
randa and has attempted to reconstruct as accurately
and objectively as possible the circumstances which led
to the sinking of the ship.

A study of the circumstances which surrounded the
last sortie of the *Scharnhorst*—the attitude of the High
Command for instance and the ship's own limited
potentialities compared with the resources available to
the British—will demonstrate how gravely the outcome
of the battle was prejudiced from the outset.

For a better understanding of the motives which
prompted this last operation it is necessary to recall
briefly the German military situation, which had deteriorated badly since the beginning of 1943.

The February of that year had brought one of the
most ominous events of the war, the fall of Stalingrad.
In spite of U-boat attack and Luftwaffe activity, the
Allies were successfully supplying the Russians with vast
quantities of war material. Within two weeks of the
arrival of each heavily laden Arctic convoy in Murmansk, the German forces on the Eastern Front would
become painfully aware of the rising power of their

adversaries. The deployment of heavy naval forces against these convoys had become a subject of lively discussion among the men at the front as well as with the Supreme Command.

Grand-Admiral Dönitz himself, after his appointment as Commander-in-Chief of the Navy, on 30 January 1943, at once advocated with the greatest emphasis the use of heavy naval units at every possible opportunity. His attitude deliberately and defiantly discounted the probable consequence of risking the few remaining heavy ships in this way. There was indeed no lack of weighty arguments against adopting such a course.

It was to be assumed that the British were well aware of the weakness of the German naval forces in the extreme north. It was equally certain that they realized why German naval forces—and heavy units at that— were stationed in northern Norwegian waters. The Germans, for their part, knew that the enemy would not be disposed to give them any opportunities for cheap success. The Arctic convoys were of vital strategic importance, and it was to be expected that they would be covered by strong forces. An absolute enemy superiority, that is to say, heavy British units operating in the same waters as the convoys, had to be reckoned with. But even so, success was not out of the question. If it proved possible to elude heavy British units and to by-pass or overcome the normal force covering a convoy, then the risk would be justified.

Nevertheless, further objections could still be raised to exposing the heavy German units to such hazards. German air reconnaissance was inadequate, a fact as disquieting as the almost total lack of bomber and fighter cover in this area. The first deficiency implied constant exposure to unpleasant surprise moves, while the second meant that no support by the Luftwaffe would be forthcoming even in an extreme emergency.

The number of naval forces available for reconnaissance sweeps was also far too small, a fact made more serious through the total lack of naval aviation. The frequent change of personnel on some of the ships aggravated matters still further and was the reason for the low standard of training among the crews. Many of the men now in service had no experience of the sea whatsoever, and there was little or no opportunity to give them the necessary training.

A further and fundamental objection was that winter was the worst conceivable time for heavy units to engage in operations in the extreme north. In the almost un-broken polar darkness the big ships would be constantly exposed to all the hazards of a night encounter. In these latitudes in winter the daylight lasts only two hours and the sun never rises above the horizon. It is perpetual night, faintly lit by an uncertain twilight. All experi-ence to date suggested that it was scarcely possible to liquidate a convoy's escort in time for the convoy itself still to be tackled during the remaining hours of twi-light, and the depleted forces now available were hope-lessly inadequate for the twofold task of tying down or destroying the enemy's covering forces while at the same time disposing of the convoy itself. In these circum-stances an encounter with enemy forces would inevitably extend into a night battle, and the experts had consis-tently held that battleships should on no account be involved in such a mêlée, for the superiority of the torpedo-carrying escort vessels would in a nocturnal encounter be decisive in favour of the British.

Of lesser moment, and affecting both sides equally, was the meteorological factor. The Arctic weather was characterized by quick changes; sudden and severe storms brought heavy snowfalls, extreme cold and exceptionally high seas.

The last and weightiest argument against throwing

the big ships into the conflict was known only to a few.
It concerned the British Radar equipment. Intelligence
reports indicated that the British already had Radar
fire-control. As the German guns could fire by Radar
to only a very limited extent, a night encounter—if this
alarming report were true—would expose the German
units practically blindfold to the accurate fire of their
opponents.

Yet in spite of all these considerations, which were of
course duly weighed in the balance by the Navy and
Naval High Command, Grand-Admiral Dönitz still
held that the heavy units should be used, a grave decision forced by the overall strategic picture and above all
the situation on the Eastern Front.

The military position had in fact progressively
deteriorated as the year wore on. Now—in December
1943—it had become well-nigh desperate. It was not
only that the Army was being forced into a continuous
and costly retreat with the successive abandonment of
front-line positions, but at many places along the far-
flung Eastern Front the Russian offensive was rolling on
irresistibly. The dangerously weakened ranks of the
battle-worn infantry, skeletons of former divisions, and
the frighteningly reduced armoured formations were
little more than dark clusters of desperately fighting
men lost in the immense wastes of the Russian winter.

The Supreme Command at Führer Headquarters
realized that something must be done to relieve the
crushing pressure on the Eastern Front. The badly
mauled Luftwaffe was almost impotent. Successes in
U-boat warfare too had been steadily falling since
February of the same year (1943). But there were still
the heavy naval units. There was still the 1st Battle
Group high up in northern Norway—the *Scharnhorst*!

Of the other big ships none was available for action
against the Arctic convoys. The *Tirpitz* was shackled to

her anchorage in Kaa Fjord inside Alta Fjord following an attack by British midget submarines. The *Gneisenau* had been seriously damaged by mines and bombs and lay out of commission in Gotenhaven. The remainder —*Prinz Eugen, Hipper, Lützow* and *Scheer*—were needed in the Baltic. But with the *Scharnhorst* and her screen of five destroyers an attack on the Arctic convoys might be possible.

The Commander-in-Chief of the 1st Battle Group, Admiral Kummertz, was on leave in Germany at this time and Rear-Admiral Bey, Commodore of Destroyers, was appointed Acting Commander-in-Chief in his place. He had never before commanded heavy units, but as a successful Commander of destroyer flotillas, he enjoyed absolute confidence and universal respect.

Meanwhile, the idea of bringing the 1st Battle Group into action had gained ground. On the occasion of one of the so-called Führer Conferences (that of 19 and 20 December 1943 at Wolfsschanze in Eastern Prussia) the Grand-Admiral took the initiative. Dönitz, who was acutely aware of the desperate need for support on the Eastern Front and wished above all that the Navy should make an all-out effort to help in some way, made a statement which startled everyone present. He announced that the *Scharnhorst* and a few escorting destroyers would attack the next convoy from Halifax to Russia passing along the northern route if a favourable opportunity presented itself. He added that it would be worth while increasing the number of U-boats operating in the northern area if the convoys showed signs of making regular use of the northern route once more. During the summer of 1943 no Arctic convoys had sailed to Murmansk. He, Dönitz, had already given orders that additional U-boats be sent into Arctic waters.

# III

## "J.W. CONVOY EN ROUTE FOR MURMANSK"

ON the morning of 24 December 1943, Christmas Eve, a report reached the Naval High Command that the long-expected J.W. convoy to Murmansk was at sea. (J.W. convoys were those that ran north-eastward to Russia; R.A. convoys those returning empty from Russia.)

Ships had actually been sighted by air reconnaissance on December 22nd—more will be said of these reports later—but the information was not sufficiently precise to suggest that the reported cargo ships necessarily represented an Arctic convoy. It was not until the Christmas Eve report came in that all doubt about this was removed.

The path of these convoys lay along the so-called northern route by Greenland, Iceland, Spitzbergen and around North Cape to Murmansk, the Russian port on the Murman coast of Lapland. The British Navy supplied the covering forces. In the convoy itself were usually destroyers, frigates, corvettes and patrol ships as a U-boat screen, all of them small ships; in addition, a line of heavy and light cruisers ran parallel to the convoy on its exposed flank, i.e. to the southward of the route, from which direction any possible German attack could be expected to come. These cruisers served as covering force against surface attack; they remained detached from the convoy itself and stood ready to intervene in an emergency. The number of freighters sailing in an Arctic convoy might be anything from twenty-five to thirty—sometimes even more—and the war material that they carried, mainly armour and heavy weapons, including ammunition, amounting on an average to half a million gross register tons, was of incalculable value.

If the *Scharnhorst* could succeed in turning the flank of the covering forces she could do more damage in a few hours than the entire U-boat fleet had been able to inflict on enemy merchant shipping in the closing months of 1943.

The first news of the convoy came in from U-boats and reconnaissance aircraft which had been actively searching for it and were now shadowing it. Actually—a fact unknown to the German High Command—there were at the time of the report two convoys at sea. One, the reported J.W.55 B convoy proceeding eastward with nineteen fully laden cargo ships, and the other, convoy R.A.55 A, sailing westward from Russia. With its 22 empty ships the latter had already passed Bear Island between Spitzbergen and North Cape without having been spotted.

On receipt of the report, Dönitz gave the 1st Battle Group, *Scharnhorst* and her five destroyers, the order to attack. The convoy's position, cruising speed and course were roughly established by the—admittedly patchy—reconnaissance reports of the U-boats and aircraft.

A south-westerly gale was blowing in the operational area. A heavy sea had come up while dense snow squalls seriously reduced visibility. The term "heavy sea" as used by seamen meant waves up to thirty feet high. They rolled up in long roaring swells, dark, foam-flecked, white crested. The gale tore sheets of spray from the crests and shot them flat across the water. The eddying snow was thicker and heavier than the men had ever known it before either in the North Sea or the North Atlantic, and it was cold as the icy breath of the

Pole itself. Such was the weather in which the convoy was sailing.

Group North/Navy were aware of the adverse weather conditions, but they had as yet no knowledge of the Grand-Admiral's recent decision to use the Battle Group for the relief of the Eastern Front in spite of all the arguments there were against this policy. The Chief of the Fleet, Admiral Schniewind, was himself doubtful of the wisdom of such a course of action not only because of the generally recognized objections but also in view of the weather conditions prevailing at the time. He attempted to persuade his superiors at Naval High Command to sanction at least a postponement of the action.

It was an extraordinarily difficult decision for the High Command to take. However, the Acting Commander-in-Chief of the Battle Group itself, Rear-Admiral Bey, appeared to be confident enough, and the Grand-Admiral finally decided in favour of the operation. He was also influenced by the U-boat and air reconnaissance reports which suggested that the convoy was covered by only a few cruisers and the usual smaller craft, i.e. vessels which in normal circumstances would have been far inferior to the *Scharnhorst*. The Grand-Admiral felt that here was a unique opportunity to give some really effective help to the hard-pressed Eastern Front and he was determined, come what may, to make the most of it.

Taking into consideration the last reported position of the convoy, Admiral Schniewind ordered the sailing of the *Scharnhorst* and the five destroyers for Christmas Day, December 25th, at 1700 hours. The Commander-in-Chief of the Battle Group, Rear-Admiral Bey, passed on the order to prepare for sea to the units in his command.

Rear-Admiral Bey was a man of massive build, an

D

excellent seaman and a born destroyer commander. A soft heart beat behind a rather forbidding exterior. In the course of the war he had, as his own men put it, "wangled some tough jobs" and he had not set foot in a battleship since his time as a young midshipman. But he had—characteristic of most commanders of small ships—a genuine understanding and sympathy for his men, and his men had the utmost confidence in him. As a commodore of destroyers he was quite accustomed to contact with the enemy; least of all would he be concerned about adverse weather; he would take it for granted that his destroyers would fight no matter what the conditions.

# IV

## THE *SCHARNHORST* PUTS TO SEA

THE darkness of Christmas Day 1943 lay over Alta Fjord. Up in northern Norway between Tromsoe and Hammerfest there was at this time of the year almost perpetual night. The waters of the fjord were blue-black and icy cold. For some days past a south-westerly gale had been sweeping over the snow-covered mountains. It hurled itself down the steep cliffs on the south shore of Lang Fjord, a western arm of Alta Fjord, as a fall-wind, and whipped up the normally calm waters of the fjord into whirls of white foam. Isolated firs, their branches bent beneath their load of snow, stood mute and motionless to half-way up the steep mountain slopes. The Northern Lights shimmered faintly in the north-western sky.

In the various lateral branches of the broad Alta Fjord lay the units of the First Battle Group. The Flag Officer, Rear-Admiral Bey, and his staff were on board the *Tirpitz*, which had been put out of active service by British midget submarines and now lay in Kaa Fjord, the innermost south-western tip of Alta Fjord proper. The *Scharnhorst*, lying athwart the fjord and riding head to the wind, had anchored at the western tip of Lang Fjord. Likewise in Lang Fjord, but a little further towards the inner end, lay the three destroyers of the 4th Destroyer Flotilla, Z 29, Z 34 and Z 38. In Kaa Fjord, the anchorage of the *Tirpitz*, lay the two remaining destroyers of the 4th Flotilla, Z 30 and Z 33.

On board the ships all traces of the Christmas Eve just past, which officers and men had as usual celebrated together, had been removed. The Christmas trees in flats and messes had disappeared and all the decorations had been taken down. In the *Scharnhorst* there was much animated conversation as rumour and conjecture passed from one part of the ship to another. Readiness for sea had been ordered for 1900 hours! It had been a long time since the *Scharnhorst* had sailed on a sortie, and the seaman loves change as much as he hates enforced idleness. There can be no doubt that the maintenance of a constant state of preparedness throughout a long period of inactivity imposes a great strain which tends to stifle enthusiasm and lower morale, and it is easy to appreciate with what relief and jubilation the order to sail was received.

Every man on board knew that something was in the air, but only the Admiral and his staff in the *Tirpitz*, the Captain of the *Scharnhorst* and a few who had to be briefed in advance of the general promulgation, knew exactly what was afoot. The wireless telegraphy and signals personnel had assumed their most secretive air. Curious glances followed Chief Navigating Boatswain Jürgens as he hurried from the Captain's rooms to the bridge, his arms full of charts. On the upper deck and in the engine-room sailing preparations were in hand. The watch on the bridge was observing the destroyers as they prepared for sea. Morse signals flickered from bridge to bridge through the blue-screened flash-lamps.

The origin of this feverish activity lay in a series of wireless messages which had been coming in since December 21st. The Battle Group, which on December 21st had been at six hours' notice for steam, received on December 22nd through Admiral Nordmann, the Admiral North Sea, who, so far as the 1st Battle Group was concerned, acted purely as intermediary, the order: "Battle Group three hours' notice for steam!"

A report from the Air Officer Commanding, North

West, finally set matters in train. This report stated that on the same day at 1045 hours about 400 miles west of Trondhjem, a weather plane had sighted a convoy of presumably forty troop ships and escort vessels steaming on a course of 45° at a speed of 10 knots. Later, when the aircraft had returned to base, the Air Officer Commanding reported that a full evaluation of the reconnaissance suggested that the convoy did not consist of troop ships but of cargo vessels of between 2,000 and 3,000 gross register tons. Then, for a time, contact with the convoy was lost. On December 23rd at 1123 hours the convoy was again picked up: course 30°, speed 10 knots. The report confirmed that they were probably not forty troop ships but seventeen cargo ships and three tankers, proceeding in seven columns, with an escort of three to four cruisers, nine destroyers and corvettes.

The Battle Group Command was at first inclined to think that this might be a landing operation against northern Norway, but later corrected the report to the effect that the convoy was one of the Arctic convoys bound for Murmansk.

A further reconnaissance report coming in at 1214 hours stated that one cruiser and five destroyers steering an easterly course had been observed east of the convoy. The view that the sighted vessels were indeed a convoy en route to Russia was thus confirmed. At this stage the Commodore of U-boats, Norway, who was also working on the assumption that a Russia-bound convoy was at sea, took a hand. He ordered the eight U-boats of Group Eisenbart which were already at sea to make a reconnaissance sweep to the west of Bear Island. On the afternoon of Christmas Eve, at 1400 hours, another report reached the 1st Battle Group. It came from the Air Officer Commanding Lofoten and it gave the position of the convoy at 1220 hours by the exact square on the squared chart, as steaming a course of 50° at a speed of eight knots. This report made it absolutely certain that the sighted ships were in fact an enemy convoy bound for Russia.

At ten o'clock on Christmas morning a reconnaissance aircraft again gave the position of the convoy, and one of the eight U-boats under Kapitänleutnant Hansen signalled that the convoy had passed over it at 0900 hours. It gave the position according to the squared chart and the course at 60°. These last two reports prompted the Commander-in-Chief of the 1st Battle Group at 1215 hours to order the *Scharnhorst* and the 4th Destroyer Flotilla to be ready at one hour's notice. At 1420 hours U-boat Hansen again reported the convoy: "Convoy AB 6723 [squared chart], course 60°, speed 8 knots. Weather: south 7, rain, visibility 2 miles."

It was at this point that the Commander of Group North/Navy, Admiral Schniewind, tried to get the authority of the Supreme Command to postpone the operation in view of the, in his opinion, inadequate air reconnaissance and the extremely unfavourable weather. But when the strained situation on the Eastern Front was again impressed upon him he withdrew his objections and on behalf of Group North/Navy, i.e. the authority superior to the Battle Group, gave the decisive signal with the prearranged code word: "Eastern Front 25.12." The order was to be interpreted: "Action of the 1st Battle Group against the convoy on the day stated, i.e. December 25th." It was received at 1415 hours and was amplified one hour later by the message: "Eastern Front 1700 hours." Actually the sailing was postponed for two hours as the Commander-in-Chief, Rear-Admiral Bey, and his staff who were in the *Tirpitz*, had to transfer to the *Scharnhorst*.

In Hammerfest, to the north-east of Alta Fjord, lay

two motor mine-sweepers of the 5th mine-sweeper flotilla, R 56 commanded by Lieutenant Wilhelm Maclot and R 58 by Sub-Lieutenant Werner Hauss.

These two boats received a wireless order at 1500 hours on Christmas Day: "Proceed at once to *Scharnhorst*. Mine-sweeping escort to Point Lucie."

Point Lucie lay north-west of Hasvik, to the west of Söröya Island, and was one extremity of a declared mined area through which the 1st Battle Group, the *Scharnhorst* and her five destroyers, had to pass on their way to the open sea. The boats, both of the Voith-Schneider type, cast off and sailed out. A strong south-westerly gale was blowing and the two commanders were dubious even at that time about the success of the operation.

But orders are orders and the darkened boats in line ahead proceeded at high speed to Alta Fjord. It was a stretch of water they had covered often enough and they knew it like the back of their hands. But there was one point that was navigationally difficult: the entrance to Lang Fjord (the western lateral arm of Alta Fjord) was closed by a barrier of steel mesh, at the far end of which the *Scharnhorst* and three of her destroyers lay at anchor. In the weather conditions then prevailing this barrier with its small black buoys was difficult to locate. A tiny trawler on patrol duty was anchored off-shore in readiness to open the barrage when called to do so. The night of this December 25th was tolerably clear and starlit, but it was nevertheless pitch dark and there was no moon. Faint spectral Northern Lights were visible in the north-western sky as the mine-sweepers steered towards the entrance to Lang Fjord. As they neared the barrier they observed that an unusually high sea was running in the fjord. The gale sweeping in from the south-west had produced fall-winds down the northern slopes of the 2,000-foot mountains which skirted the fjord to the south. Dammed up by the equally steep rock walls on the northern shore opposite, they chopped the waters in the outer and central part of Lang Fjord into a wildly confused cross-sea. These fall-winds are typical of the inner fjords and also of the indented coastline and are called in Norwegian *Sno* or *Elvegust*. They bring about drastic falls in temperature and their furious impact whips the normally calm waters of the fjords into "dust" or *Havrög*. The drop in temperature which accompanies the fall-winds is due to the fact that cold air-masses, accumulated on the high plateaux or beyond the mountains, are sucked down into the valley. In this witches' cauldron of foam and spray the steel-mesh barrier and buoys could not be seen, but the leading mine-sweeper R 56 commanded by the senior officer, Lieutenant Maclot, managed to find and pass through the very narrow entry gap which the patrol trawler had opened after being summoned by a morse lamp.

However, the men aboard R 58, which was following the leading boat at a distance of 200 yards, found suddenly that they could distinguish nothing whatsoever. The Captain, Bridge Petty Officer, Signalman and the two look-outs at starboard and port tried in vain to locate the patrol vessel which they knew must be lying somewhere off-shore in the shadow of the cliffs.

"*Verdammter Mist!*" cursed the young Captain, and without lowering the heavy night-glasses he spoke to the Quartermaster of the watch:

"Can *you* see anything? Where the devil is that net tender?"

"Can't see a thing, Sir. But we must be quite close to the barrier."

Just as the Captain was lowering his glasses to scan the white-foaming waters immediately ahead, the port look-out called:

"Barrage right ahead, Herr Leutnant!"

Immediately ahead of the mine-sweeper a few black buoys were bobbing up and down, barely visible in the dim starlight and continually washed over by the high seas that transfigured the calm waters of the fjord.

"Ten astern", rang out the Captain's order.

Below the bridge, in confined sheltered quarters which also housed the R.T. Wireless Operator, the man on duty pushed two levers back from "ahead", past zero to "10 astern".

The Voith-Schneider boats had neither rudder nor screw. They were steered and their speed was regulated by altering the position of the "knives" in relation to the rotating sheave or disc into which the knives fitted, hanging down vertically. The engines propelling the disc maintained the same number of revolutions. Changes of course were made by altering the so-called "gradient". This gradient extended from "zero" to "10 ahead or astern", and was marked on the dials. The position "stop" did not exist with the Voith-Schneider boats, only "zero". The usual steering orders still applied, but there was no actual rudder; everything was done by the "knives". This meant that a Voith-Schneider boat could turn in her own length, dog-fashion, without gathering either head or stern way. Such boats started more gently and at the same time with greater impetus than those equipped with the normal type of screw. Nor was it necessary for rapid steering to put one of the gradients ahead and the other astern. This was quite superfluous with vessels of such high manœuvrability.

The watch then, sensing the extreme danger of the situation, threw the levers back to "10 astern". This called for considerable effort as the lever action was stiff. Although the boat responded at once, every man on the bridge felt the soft jerk, familiar to every seaman, of a boat running aground. The Captain bent low over the bridge's guard-rails; the boat was stuck fast in the net up to practically half her length.

The Sub-Lieutenant swore under his breath as he observed the boat's attempts to disentangle herself. Slowly, very slowly, she pulled astern. Another jerk and they were clear. The edge of the net and the buoys had swung forward. With a sigh of relief the Commander readjusted his U-boat type life-jacket.

"Thank God! Zero . . . 10 ahead . . . hard a-starboard along the net barrage."

He raised his night-glasses and looked around.

"That's the trawler over there—and the entry gap as well . . . hard a-port!"

They passed through the gap, proceeded at half speed into Lang Fjord and shaped course towards the inner end of the narrowing waters. At last a great shadow rose ghost-like out of the surrounding darkness which, within the fjord, seemed even more impenetrable.

"It's the *Scharnhorst*, Sir," reported the Petty Officer. "She's lying with her port bow fine into the wind, athwart the fjord. Three destroyers behind her."

"Yes, I can see her," murmured the Captain, "and R 56 is lying on her port side."

It was about 1700 hours when R 58 went alongside R 56 and made fast.

The dead calm within the fjord seemed strange after the wild seething waters outside. The three destroyers, all carefully blacked-out, were lying towards the inner end of the fjord. There was not a glimmer of light, not a sound: only the quick phantom-like flicker of a violet-blue morse lamp showed now and again from the high bridge of the battleship in the direction of the destroyers. The dark snow-covered mountains soared heavenwards, the starry sky faintly illuminated by the ghostly glancing streaks of the Northern Lights. The calm seemed unreal, dream-like, almost uncanny.

In spite of the cold Lieutenant Maclot took off his leather jacket, revealing his newly won German Cross. Leaning over the guard-rail of the bridge, he shouted:

"Hey there, Hauss! We've got to report at once to the Captain of the big fellow. Hurry up, man. Where have you been all this time?"

"I couldn't find the barrage-gap, what with the darkness and that damned cross-sea. I got the net . . ."

"All right," the senior officer cut him short. "Now ten ahead, man."

Lieutenant Maclot scaled the flimsy ladder to the deck of the battleship, with Hauss following close behind. They were both ill at ease. They had never set foot in such a big ship before, monstrous in her proportions and confusing in her complexity. They felt themselves to be the true seamen, sovereigns of their small weather-wise craft; they were not used to being cogs in a great machine. A little embarrassed by their surroundings they reported to the officer on duty and the First Officer-of-the-Watch. The latter summoned a Sub-Lieutenant.

"Will you take the Captains to the C.O. please?"

The two men exchanged surreptitious grins. They had been referred to as "Captains". No matter whether one commanded a mine-sweeper or a battleship, a Captain was a Captain, an officer flying his own pennant, that long, narrow, white pennant with the small iron cross on the inner bolt-rope. They followed the Sub-Lieutenant across the quarterdeck, which seemed endless. They were hustled down companionways, along warm, narrow passages, past a row of officers' cabins, round corners and along more passages. By the time they were at the Captain's cabin, they had lost all sense of direction. The Sub-Lieutenant knocked briefly and opened the door for them.

They exchanged surprised glances. By their standards

the apartment was positively princely. They saluted and
remained unobtrusively in the background wondering
what would come next. The Captain, the First Officer
and the Chief Engineer were standing in the centre of
the room. The Adjutant was there too with a wireless
message in his hand. The Captain was addressing the
Chief Engineer, and the mine-sweeper captains were
just in time to catch the last few words:

"... preparations for sea must accordingly be acceler-
ated. We sail at 1800 hours."

On the Commander's desk, near which the officers
were gathered, lay the battle order of the Commander-
in-Chief of the Battle Group, Rear-Admiral Bey, which
was to be handed over by an officer to the leader of the
Destroyer Flotilla when anchors were weighed. The
*Scharnhorst* had already received her orders, contained
in a sealed envelope which was to be opened after sailing. They comprised seven points:

1. Enemy situation.
2. Own battle forces.
3. Task.
4. Intention.
5. Instructions for performing the task.
6. Instructions for the *Tirpitz* (which was to remain
   behind).
7. Signalling arrangements.

The *Task* was the destruction of the reported convoy,
and it was the Commander-in-Chief's *Intention* to proceed in accordance with an order of Group North/Navy
which made the following provisions:

(*a*) Action of the First Battle Group, consisting of the
   *Scharnhorst* and five destroyers, against the convoy on December 26th at dawn, i.e. at about
   1000 hours.
(*b*) Battle line in close order only if battle conditions

were favourable, i.e. tolerable weather conditions with good visibility, permitting a full appreciation of the enemy's dispositions.

(c) If the tactical situation was not favourable for the *Scharnhorst*, the destroyers were to attack alone, the battleship standing by to pick up the destroyers while remaining herself at a distance from the target area. If necessary she was to withdraw to the outer fjord.

In the case of (c), however, the Rear-Admiral intended to deviate from the order of Group North/Navy by keeping not only the *Scharnhorst* but the entire Battle Group, that is to say, the battleship and the destroyers, away from the target area. Having regard to the possibly concentrated fire-power of the British escort, the destroyers were not to attack until the onset of total darkness. Alternatively, should more favourable conditions obtain on December 27th, the *Scharnhorst* and five destroyers were to attack simultaneously at early dawn, that is, at about 1000 hours.

While the Captain of the *Scharnhorst* was giving further instructions to two of his own officers—Fregattenkapitän Dominik and Korvettenkapitän König—the mine-sweeper commanders took a discreet look round. There were comfortable arm-chairs, paintings on the walls, framed photographs on the desk and—it suddenly caught the eye of the Sub-Lieutenant, Hauss—a festively decorated dish of Christmas fare. Of course, he thought, it's Christmas Day! If I hadn't seen this bowl of fruit and nuts and sweet things with its sprigs of fir and tinsel ribbon, I'd have quite forgotten. He was still immersed in nostalgic thoughts of Christmas when he became aware that Captain Hintze was advancing towards him and his companion. They introduced themselves.

"So you're the Captains of the mine-sweepers? *Danke sehr*. The First Officer will give you details."

The First Officer nodded and motioned the two men to follow him to his cabin. As they were about to leave the Captain called the senior of the two commanders over to him.

"One moment, please."

He took a letter from a drawer of his desk and handed it to the Lieutenant.

"Would you be good enough—I'm afraid I did not catch your name . . ."

"Maclot, Herr Kapitän."

"Thank you, Maclot. Would you post this letter for me? Our own mail has already left."

"With pleasure, Herr Kapitän. It shall be done," and the Lieutenant put the white envelope in his pocket.

They took their leave and followed the First Officer into his cabin. The apartment was roomy and comfortable. A large-framed family picture stood on the well-equipped writing-desk which was heaped with papers. A barograph on a mahogany base stood under the port-holes which sported gay curtains. A book-case stood against the wall. The First Officer invited the two men to be seated and they sank into the unfamiliar luxury of the easy-chairs. The Fregattenkapitän murmured an apology and glanced briefly through some papers that had accumulated during his absence. Then he turned to the mine-sweeper officers:

"I should just like to run quickly through the technical details. What is your maximum speed?"

"Sixteen knots, Herr Kapitän," answered the Lieutenant.

"And with your gear out?"

The Lieutenant hesitated a moment. "Fourteen knots, Herr Kapitän."

He pondered whether he should qualify his statement by adding that this speed held good for normal weather conditions but would be quite out of the question in the storm which was raging outside at that moment. But he said nothing. It seemed to him almost certain that the operation would have to be called off and that the mine-sweepers would not be put into service. He decided to keep his thoughts about the prevailing weather to himself. Even these big-ship men, he reflected, not without disdain, must surely realize what it was like outside. The clipped, clear, authoritative voice of the First Officer broke in upon his thoughts:

"Further details will follow. As you can see, I've a great deal to attend to before sailing. Would you please see the Signals Officer now?"

He pressed a button and a messenger entered.

"Please take these gentlemen to the Signals Officer."

A quick handshake and the mine-sweeper captains were dismissed.

"They don't seem to have much time for us in this old tub," whispered Maclot to his companion as they hurried after the messenger. It was hard work keeping up with him as he sped through what seemed a veritable labyrinth of gangways, past doors, companionways, flats, workshops, gun sub-structures, telephones, control posts, then more passages, steep iron stairways, cables and never-ending rows of compartments. They felt hopelessly lost Maclot, panting behind the rating who went ahead at the double without once looking behind him, called out at length:

"Hey, stay with us, old man, or we'll never find our way out. What's the hurry, anyway?"

What struck both men on this their first visit on board a battleship was the hectic rush, the feverish activity everywhere. The place was like a disturbed ant-heap. Every man they met looked as if he was on some vital errand, engaged in a race against time. What they, as mine-sweeper men, did not realize was that this was a quite normal state of affairs on a battleship preparing for sea. Stumbling over some potato sacks which were stacked in a narrow passage-way, they arrived at last at the W/T office, where they met the Signals Officer, Kapitänleutnant Behr. Here again there was not much to discuss. The two mine-sweeper captains were old hands and knew their job. They had sailed on mine-sweeping escort countless times, in company with battle-ships, cruisers, destroyers and—their most frequent task —small convoys in the North Sea and the Channel, in waters from Skudesnes to North Cape and through the maze of fjords along the northern coast of Norway. To Narvik, Tromsoe, Hammerfest. To Kirkenes and Petsamo, running the gauntlet of the many Russian shore batteries on the Fischer peninsula and the bomb-ing attacks of Russian aircraft, making for the entrance to Petsamo harbour under cover of their own smoke-screen and never failing to get there.

"How are we going to keep in touch?" asked Maclot.

"R/T of course," was the short answer. "Verbal communication."

This meant radio-telephony from ship to ship; the mine-sweepers had the necessary R/T equipment on board. A few more questions, a few more explanations, and they were once more dismissed. As they emerged from the W/T office they observed with satisfaction that the messenger had waited for them and was ready to guide them safely back to the upper deck. They did not know anyone on board and in the general upheaval no one thought to offer them a drink—as would certainly have been the case in more normal circumstances. So they took their leave and descended to their own ships.

They had been on board the battleship for little more than half an hour but they were both glad when they were sitting down again in the cramped quarters of their own modest craft and their respective stewards appeared with supper. "Never again!" they thought, as they reached for the *Schnaps* (which they kept under lock and key in the action locker) and poured themselves a stiff drink.

For two hours, from about 1700 to 1900, the minesweepers lay alongside the battleship, but received no further orders or instructions. Sub-Lieutenant Hauss was taking his ease in his bunk with a book, enjoying an unexpected rest, when a signalman reported:

"R 121, Herr Leutnant, has gone alongside the *Scharnhorst* with a party of men on board."

The Sub-Lieutenant jumped to his feet, frowning.

"Taken some men to the *Scharnhorst*? Who could they be? Where can they have come from?"

"I don't know, Sir. But they say there's a pilot among them, and a meteorologist."

The Sub-Lieutenant looked puzzled.

"That's strange. But it doesn't really matter. Thank you!"

R 121 with Chief Quartermaster Horst Stobka, specially summoned from Tromsoe, on board, had in fact transferred the Admiral himself and his staff from the *Tirpitz* to the *Scharnhorst*. But the mine-sweeper commander did not discover this until eight years later.

Shortly before 1900 hours—the Captain of R 58 having dozed off on his hard bunk—a voice from the *Scharnhorst's* bridge, amplified by megaphone, startled the mine-sweeper men:

"Mine-sweepers cast off!"

The young captains were on their bridges in an instant. A few blasts on the battery whistles and ropes were unbent, hauled in and coiled down. The boats, lean and elegant, slid back noiselessly. Running for a few seconds almost alongside, they withdrew in a short arc. They were a well-practised team: there was no need for loud commands; they proceeded seaward almost like

**E**

phantoms. Then they stopped and waited for further instructions. Two small tugs became visible and approached the battleship. The fjord here was narrow and constricted. The *Scharnhorst*, lying head into the wind and athwart the fjord, had first to be swung round by the tugs before she could make for the barrage-gap of Lang Fjord under her own steam. At the same time, shortly before 1900 hours, the *Scharnhorst's* loudspeaker system was heard ordering the crew to the quarter-deck. The First Officer was to give orders for the start of the operation.

The men came scurrying aft from the living quarters in the battery and lower decks, from store rooms, cabins and wardrooms. They realized that at last the veil of secrecy was to be lifted and they would know why the sailing order had been given. Gradually the tramping of the many seaboots subsided as the men reported to their respective officers. They stood there in silence and waited in two long dark blocks. Passing by the heavy after-turret a tall, slender figure approached. It was Fregattenkapitän Dominik, the First Officer. He had been on board the *Scharnhorst* ever since she had been commissioned, and was an experienced gunnery expert who had risen from the rank of Captain of A.A. guns to First Gunnery Officer before he was appointed First Officer. A man of unshakeable composure, he had throughout his years of service in the *Scharnhorst* taken a personal interest in his men and was particularly popular with them. They looked at him expectantly as, the most senior officer having duly reported, he mounted the rostrum and began his short address: "On behalf of the Captain I have to inform the ship's company ..." The *Scharnhorst*, the men were told, had been ordered to attack a convoy and if possible destroy it. The convoy was heavily laden and on its way to Russia. The *Scharnhorst* was sailing with five destroyers in order to relieve, by attacking the convoy, the crushing pressure on the Eastern Front.

The words of the final order to prepare for action had hardly left his lips before general jubilation broke out. Spontaneous cheers echoed across the fjord, while the enthusiastic men—discipline for the moment forgotten—hoisted the First Officer on to their shoulders and carried him forward. Then the men rushed to their action stations. Within three minutes—record time—all stations were reported clear for action. Captain Hintze, who received the report from the First Officer on the bridge, raised his hand to his cap in appreciation. "Everything is possible with a crew like ours, Dominik," he said quietly.

As the First Officer went to the forecastle for weighing the anchor a motor-boat, coming in from the outer fjord, glided across the smooth water. Her wake glimmered faintly through the darkness. The last of the *Scharnhorst* men were on board; they were the depth-charge crew who had been standing by in the outer fjord, on guard against the possible penetration of British midget submarines, whose reappearance since their successful attack on the *Tirpitz* had constantly to be reckoned with. Oberbootsmannsmaat Gödde—one of the later survivors—was their leader. The boat went alongside the *Scharnhorst*, the men climbed on board and the Captain immediately gave the order to weigh anchor.

For the last time the capstan revolved and the heavy chain cable rattled through the hawsepipe. Then the engine-room telegraphs crackled their "Stand by" while the two tugs nosed the great ship at bow and stern. The engine-room telegraphs crackled again, the tugs cut free and the disturbed waters of the fjord boiled up about the stern. The *Scharnhorst* swung round and then headed down Lang Fjord towards the net barrage. For the mine-sweeper captains who watched silently from their bridges, this was an unforgettable sight: the long slender shadow of the handsomely proportioned ship gliding past and slowly gathering speed, without light, without sound. Beautiful and lethal, she came speeding from her mountain lair to hunt in the open.

The mine-sweepers, having received no further orders, formed astern the battleship, R 58 tailing R 56. Blue-screened morse lamps from the high bridge of the *Scharnhorst* flickered over to the destroyers. Z 29, the leading destroyer, answered. Then destroyer Z 38 swept nearer, rushed past the mine-sweepers, overtook the *Scharnhorst*, and dropped into station six cables ahead of the battleship to assist in navigation up to the barrage. The other two destroyers, Z 29 and Z 34, took up station in the *Scharnhorst's* wake. Suddenly the mine-sweepers picked up an R/T order. The signalman in the room obliquely before and below the bridge of R 58 received the order and reported:

"Speed 17 knots!"

Astonished, Hauss bent down to him:

"What was that? Seventeen knots? Are you sure you got it right?"

"Certain, Sir. It's meant for the destroyers. I could hear it plainly: Seventeen knots!"

"Still no order for us," thought the Sub-Lieutenant. "Even without gear laid out we can do only sixteen knots and the First Officer on the *Scharnhorst* knows it. He asked about it himself. Still, let's see what Maclot is doing."

But R 56 was only maintaining course and was now dropping considerably behind as the battleship and her destroyers pulled away at seventeen knots. The signalman in R 58 reported further orders he had picked up. Somewhere in the darkness R 121 which likewise had received no order to detach was sailing parallel to the course of the other two mine-sweepers.

A sudden call came from the signalman:

"Herr Leutnant! R 121 has just called up the *Scharnhorst*. And she's got the bird!"

"Oh-ho!" Hauss was interested. "What did she ask?"

"I couldn't quite get it, Sir, but the answer from the *Scharnhorst* was: 'Stop cutting in'!"

The men thought it a huge joke and were glad that their own commanders had refrained from interrupting the battleship while she was in course of transmitting signals to her destroyers.

While, at 1955 hours, the First Battle Group was passing the inner Lang Fjord barrage, the mine-sweepers followed the advancing force at a considerable distance. R 58 again missed the barrage-gap in the pitch darkness and had to search for it. She found it eventually and once through, stepped up her speed. Slowly and calmly the patrol trawler shut the barrier once more and steamed back to her waiting position off shore. Still no order of dismissal had come through for the three sweepers. To port, where, after picking up the two destroyers which had sailed from Kaa Fjord and turning into Stjern Sund the Battle Group was swallowed up by darkness, faint Northern Lights still coloured the north-western sky. Nothing was to be seen of the third sweeper, R 56. Just as Hauss was wondering whether he should signal her, there was a flicker at starboard ahead.

"Call from R 56," reported the Leading Signalman.

"Reply! Flash signals to the line on the port bow," the Captain ordered with a sigh of relief. "Ten ahead!"

"She's headed for Varget Sund!" the Quartermaster noted. "Surely we shall be going back to Hammerfest, Herr Leutnant?"

The Captain shrugged his shoulders:

"No order is out yet, but I should certainly think so. Look, if . . ."

"R/T from *Scharnhorst* to the First Battle Group: Speed seventeen knots!" called the signalman.

"Well, that's as good as an order to detach," said Sub-Lieutenant Hauss. "In any case we couldn't sail with our gear out in weather like this. Certainly not to Point Lucie!"

Once again he lifted the night-glasses in the direction of the Battle Group. Nothing could be seen of it now. The six dark shadows, which shortly before had been gliding along, a shade darker than the black background of the mountainsides, had completely disappeared.

"Damn and blast!" murmured the Sub-Lieutenant and followed in his mind the route that the First Battle Group would now be taking. Ahead the busy morse-lamp of R 56 was flickering again.

"Order from R 56," reported Leading Signalman Pietz. "Follow wake. Course Hammerfest."

For the three sweepers of the Fifth Mine-Sweeper Flotilla the task was at an end.

The letter from the *Scharnhorst's* Captain, which Lieutenant Maclot handed to the post-orderly of the Flotilla for dispatch on the following morning, was to be the last news of the *Scharnhorst* to reach the homeland.

The Battle Group, cruising at 17 knots, had passed the outer barrage at 2037 hours and from 2110 hours onward steered through Stjern and Stoeroey Sunds and Lappahavet at a speed of 25 knots towards the open sea. At around 2200 hours the Admiral ordered two destroyers to come up to either side of the battleship to form a U-boat screen while the leading destroyer Z 29 was ordered to take up station ahead of the *Scharnhorst* and so form the spearhead. At 2304 hours Point Lucie was passed and at a cruising speed of 25 knots on a course of 10° the force made for the point where it was calculated the convoy could be intercepted.

In the open sea the ships were lashed by the gale and enveloped by the darkness of the Arctic night. The faintly glimmering trail of their wake was quickly dispersed and no trace was left of their passage. Coldly the stars glinted and pale Northern Lights played with their delicate green, pink and bluish-violet hues on the north-western horizon. The operation had begun.

# V

# THE ROYAL NAVY AND THE CONVOYS

WHILE German naval forces were being charged with the task of cutting the British life-line to and from Russia, the Home Fleet was being called upon to protect and defend the convoys which formed this life-line.

The vital importance of the convoy escorts can best be appreciated in relation to the enormous quantities of war material—the output of mines and factories all over the world—which each convoy carried. As already mentioned the Arctic convoys usually comprised twenty or more cargo ships, averaging from 6,000 to 8,000 b.r.t.

One gross register ton (b.r.t.) is a cubic measure corresponding to 40 cubic feet, and the interior space of a ship is expressed in b.r.t. Roughly a third of the space is taken up by the ship's machinery (boilers, engines, propeller-shafts and various other technical installations such as auxiliary engines and tiller gear), crew space and storage. The remaining two-thirds represents the net tonnage available for cargo. A single freighter of 6,000 b.r.t. carried, apart from lighter war materials such as ammunition, guns and other weapons, 18 twin-engined bombers (partly dismantled), 155 14-ton tanks and 51 28–30-ton tanks. Hence one Arctic convoy of twenty freighters carried in terms of aircraft and armour alone: 360 twin-engined bombers, 3,100 14-ton tanks and 1,020 28–30-ton tanks.

The Arctic convoys sailed round the most northerly

point of Norway to Murmansk. The farther north they kept the safer they were from attack, but their voyage took proportionately longer and this was at a time when hours could be decisive. Furthermore, the sea to the north became increasingly rougher. The wind which blew in directly from the Pole churned up mountainous seas, while visibility was obliterated in furious flurries of snow. The dark sky precluded light and it was literally impossible to see one's own hand. Only occasionally would the green-yellow or red-violet Northern Lights cast an unsteady, erratic gleam. At noon the day would turn a pale grey for about two hours although the sun never rose above the horizon. The cold was almost unbearable. Watchkeepers on warships and freighters shivered in spite of sheepskin clothing and many layers of woollens. Depth charges froze fast to the decks, gun-sights and breeches became encrusted with ice, and the lubricants on the munition-hoists froze hard. A warship which failed to take special precautions to safeguard the lives of her crew and keep her armament free of ice, could not hope to survive an action in these waters.

At the time in question, the end of 1943, the defensive power of the covering forces had grown to such an extent that attacks by U-boats and aircraft could do little more than harass the convoys; they could not stop them. There was only one thing that could have stopped them—naval superiority. If Germany had possessed superior surface forces, no convoy or single cargo-ship could have ventured into those waters; at best an odd blockade runner might have tried to break through. But Germany simply did not have that superiority; her naval forces at that time were definitely inferior. She retained, however, one formidable advantage—a base from which sorties against convoys could be launched: northern Norway.

The constant threat from German surface forces, even such as they were, particularly the heavy units stationed in northern Norway, forced the British to take onerous precautions. They, the stronger side, had to cover every convoy with escorting forces each of which had to be more powerful than the total German forces available for an attack. As the British could never predict when the First Battle Group with the *Scharnhorst* would choose to attack, they had to maintain a constant state of preparedness. This meant that the destroyers, frigates and corvettes which formed the normal protection against U-boats had always to be augmented by a squadron of heavy and light cruisers with the possible addition of heavy units, battleships and aircraft-carriers. To safeguard and escort these heavy units, a further number of cruisers and destroyers were necessary as reconnaissance forces.

These complex and costly measures, and the fatigue attendant upon continuous and extended escort duties in Arctic regions, imposed an exceptional strain on the limited personnel and shipping available. They also involved an elaborate and permanent organization for refuelling, not to mention the constant danger of losses by U-boats, bombers and surface forces.

Any failure correctly to estimate the potential danger and to take adequate precautions against it, would give the *Scharnhorst* her opportunity. If the battleship could approach a convoy unmolested she could at this season inflict more damage in the two hours of twilight than a whole U-boat flotilla could inflict in six months.

The normal covering-force, known to the Germans and in this instance reported by U-boat and air reconnaissance, consisted of small craft, destroyers, frigates, corvettes and patrol vessels which surrounded the convoy proper on every side. In addition a cruiser squadron stood to the southward, that is on the side from which a German surface attack could be expected. But what the reconnaissance forces had on this occasion not discovered was that a heavy unit consisting of one battleship, in company with one cruiser and four destroyers, was also at sea. We shall see later why this force had remained undetected. The normal convoy escort of small craft and the cruiser squadron would have been inferior to the *Scharnhorst*, which, with her superior speed, was in any event able to disengage at will.

# VI

## THE BRITISH RADAR APPARATUS

EVEN more important than the numerical strength of the escorting force, and more decisive than the squadron with the heavy unit, was Radar, or, as it was called by the Germans, the improved "Rotterdam-apparatus".

Dr Curt Bley in his book *The Radar Secret* tells how in January 1943 a British bomber was shot down near Rotterdam. In it some strange equipment was found half-destroyed. It bore an inscription hurriedly scribbled on it in pencil: "Experimental 6." The apparatus was sent to the *Telefunken* Company in Berlin-Zehlendorf for closer inspection. The scientists there established that it worked on a 9-cm. wavelength and named it the "Rotterdam-apparatus". Up to this time it had been thought that a centimetre wavelength was unsuitable for radio detection and ranging. On 9 March 1943, the Berlin-Zehlendorfer laboratories were destroyed in an air raid. The remains of "Experimental 6" were salvaged from the smouldering ruins with infinite care, and on orders from Göring, the laboratory was re-established in one of the strongest A.A. towers in Germany, the Flak-tower in Humboldt-Hain, Berlin. There an attempt was made to reconstruct "Experimental 6". Unfortunately a few essential parts were missing from the half-destroyed prototype and it was not until several weeks later, when another British aircraft carrying the same apparatus was shot down, that it could be completely reconstructed. In August 1943, the apparatus was finally mounted on the top platform of the A.A. tower.

The sight which now greeted the scientists must surely have provided one of the greatest surprises of the war. For, etched on the screen in green fluorescent light was nothing less than a complete picture of the city of Berlin with its blocks of flats, streets, squares and parks. Beyond could be seen all the environs of the city, the woods, lakes, waterways, canals and clusters of houses, to a radius of 40 miles. To the left lay the Wannsee, its outline well defined, to the right the Müggelsee, its wooded slopes clearly visible. This meant that darkness had been conquered and that whatever the weather, British bombers and British warships could observe every target as clearly as if it were on a moving film strip.

Lord Cherwell, on the occasion of its first trials, had called this magic instrument "Home, sweet home", abbreviated to "H 2 S". Further developed and improved it had been employed by bombers in battle against U-boats since the beginning of August 1943. It was fitted to all British warships and before long the British naval guns were making use of its magic eye for fire-control.

Theories put forward by German radio specialists concerning the range of this novel apparatus and its possibilities for artillery fire-control, were soon confirmed. Two German destroyers, Z 26 and *Hermann Schoemann*, had just been lost in the Arctic Ocean in mysterious circumstances. Both destroyers had served in numerous sorties against convoys and had been accustomed to operating in thick weather. Suddenly and quite unexpectedly they had been confronted by a British cruiser. At the very moment when the German look-outs had sighted the cruiser emerging from the mist as a vague shadow and had duly made their reports, the destroyers had been straddled by accurate salvoes. It was absolutely impossible that the few seconds of mutual visual sighting could have sufficed to supply the data needed for such accurate firing. The cruiser must have had some instrument by means of which the German destroyers had been sighted through the mist and which had also been able to give reliable indications as to range, etc., to the gunners. It now seemed certain that the British units were making use of Radar fire-control.

To anticipate a little, it must be assumed that neither the Commander-in-Chief of the German Battle Group, Rear-Admiral Bey, nor Captain Hintze of the *Scharnhorst* was sufficiently informed of the latest stages of Radar development—which were known only to a small circle of experts in Germany—to be able correctly to assess its far-reaching influence on naval warfare. Furthermore, although they credited their opponents with the possession of Radar they were certainly ignorant of the degree of their technical superiority in this sphere.

# VII

## ADMIRAL SIR BRUCE FRASER
## SETS THE TRAP

THE Commander-in-Chief of the British Home Fleet, Admiral Sir Bruce Fraser, was flying his flag in the battleship *Duke of York*. The small unit, known as Force 2, with which the Admiral himself sailed, comprised the battleship *Duke of York*, the light cruiser *Jamaica* and the destroyers *Savage*, *Scorpion*, *Saumarez* and *Stord*.

The Admiral himself directed operations for the protection of the Arctic convoys and the *Duke of York* was explicitly committed to corner and engage the *Scharnhorst* when opportunity arose.

Force 2 had accompanied the previous convoy J.W.55 A to Russia as far as Kola Inlet, the entrance to Kola Bay, in the central section and on the eastern shore of which lay the port of Murmansk. The Admiral had then taken his Force back to Akureyri on the north coast of Iceland, one of the bases from which the Home Fleet units covering the convoys and the warships of Western Approaches Command were operating.

It was 23 December 1943. While Force 2 was refuelling, Sir Bruce had summoned his staff and the captains of his Force to a meeting in the Admiral's room on the flagship. On the great table of the conference room a large-scale map, covering the whole area from Greenland to Murmansk, and detailed charts of the Arctic sea regions were laid out. Tables showing the maximum ranges of the various ships in the Force and their respective fuel consumption at cruising and top speeds were also to hand. Other data gave the composition and escorts of the convoys under way. The Admiral appeared and after greeting his officers lost no time in coming to the point:

"I wish to deal with preparations for covering convoy J.W.55 B," he said. "As convoy J.W.55 A, which we have just accompanied, has got through unmolested, I am convinced that the *Scharnhorst* will come out and endeavour to attack J.W.55 B. Happily our Force has now been in company for a fortnight and we are well acquainted with each other's ways. In this connexion," the Admiral added with the shadow of a smile, "the night encounter exercises which I initiated have probably had a certain value."

Upon a sign from Sir Bruce the Chief-of-Staff went up to the table, took one of the detailed charts and, assisted by the youngest destroyer captain who had quickly come forward, held it up. Taking a pair of compasses, the Chief-of-Staff described a semi-circle to the south of an island lying between the Spitzbergen Group and North Cape. They all knew it; it was Bear Island.

"The principal danger-zone," began the Chief-of-Staff, "lies to the south of Bear Island. As, unfortunately, the endurance of our destroyers," the speaker glanced almost apologetically at the four destroyer captains, "does not permit continuous cover to be given for the whole passage, our intention is to advance at a speed of fifteen knots and meet the convoy in the neighbourhood of Bear Island. This will allow the whole Force to remain for about thirty hours in the critical area. At the same time an R.A. convoy, namely R.A.55 A, is approaching Bear Island from the east. This convoy consists of twenty-two cargo ships and is escorted by eight destroyers: *Musketeer, Opportune,*

*Virago, Matchless, Milne, Meteor, Ashanti* and *Athabascan*, and by the mine-sweeper *Seagull*. In addition there are five ships of Western Approaches Command, the two destroyers *Beagle* and *Westcott* and the three corvettes *Dianella, Poppy* and *Acanthus*. Up to the present there is no indication that the enemy has detected this convoy. In any case it is unlikely to be attacked as it is returning empty from Murmansk. Nonetheless this possibility must also be taken into account."

The Chief-of-Staff replaced the chart and took up a document headed "J.W.55 B". Glancing quickly at the tabulated information it contained he continued:

"The convoy J.W.55 B which we now have to cover consists of nineteen merchant ships. It is escorted by the eight destroyers *Onslow, Onslaught, Haida, Iroquois, Orwell, Huron, Scourge* and *Impulse*, and the mine-sweeper *Gleaner*. There are in addition, from Western Approaches Command, the two destroyers *Whitehall* and *Wrestler*, and the corvettes *Honeysuckle* and *Oxlip*. At some distance from the convoy stands the 10th Cruiser Squadron commanded by Vice-Admiral Burnett, i.e. Force 1, consisting of the heavy cruiser *Norfolk* and the light cruisers *Belfast* (the flag-ship) and *Sheffield*."

The Chief-of-Staff stopped speaking and for a moment there was silence at the conference table. Only the blurred indeterminate sounds of life going on in the great ship could be heard—an announcement over the loudspeaker system, the tramp of sea-boots and, as a muffled noise from outside, the low insistent drone of a tug. The Admiral, who had been listening intently with his arms crossed behind his back, straightened himself and thrust his hands into his jacket pockets.

"Should we encounter the *Scharnhorst*," said Sir Bruce, rising slightly on to his toes, "I have decided

F

first, to close with the enemy at once and to open fire with starshell at a range of about 12,000 yards."

He paused and looked at the commander of the flagship, Captain the Hon. G. H. E. Russell. The Captain nodded gravely.

"Coming to my second point," the Admiral went on, turning to the four destroyer commanders, "I intend to form the four escorting destroyers into sub-divisions and, when the right moment comes, to release them for torpedo attack."

Commander Meyrick and the three Lieutenant-Commanders Clouston, Walmsley and Storehill instinctively squared their shoulders. It was obvious that this proposed course of action had their wholehearted approval.

"Finally, I will keep you, Captain Hughes-Hallet, with your *Jamaica*, with me. You will, however, have freedom of action, and may of course open the distance between us if I go into action with the *Duke of York*."

A low-pitched "Aye, aye, Sir!" from the cruiser Captain assured the Admiral that his order had been understood. Finally, the Admiral raised his voice:

"I have to make a last and most important point," he said. "Every man must be doubly sure he knows his night action duty. We in the Home Fleet have had drastic changes of personnel and these constant convoy duties have made regular training practically impossible. I intend tomorrow morning to carry out a last practice attack, using the *Jamaica* as target. Ready for sea tonight at 2300 hours. Thank you, gentlemen."

# VIII

## THE *DUKE OF YORK* SAILS
## WITH FORCE 2

ADMIRAL Sir Bruce Fraser accordingly sailed
with Force 2. In the small hours of December
24th they passed through the long broad Eya
Fjord (at the innermost tip of which Akureyri lies) and
reached the open sea. The island of Grimsey (off the
northern coast of Iceland) already lay well to the west
of the Force when the Admiral directed that the signal
be given for the practice attack to begin.

The light cruiser *Jamaica* hauled out of line with
gathering speed and a foaming bow-wave. Passing
abeam of the flagship *Duke of York* she slewed off,
the silhouette of her high bridge structures, her two
funnels and the two triple turrets fore and aft only
faintly discernible in the darkness of the night. The sea
broke in over her bows, hissed across the tops of the
turrets and sent lashings of spray up to the bridge. The
wind blew hard from the south-west. The slender ship,
running before the sea, began to roll heavily and soon
disappeared from the sight of the men watching from
the bridge of the flagship. The four destroyers too had
gathered headway and with a whirling stern-sea fell
into their stations. The battle practice had begun.

The Captain of the flagship, who had been studying
a wireless weather report, handed the form to his Navigating Officer:

"The sou'-wester is freshening. Looks as if we're
going to have a rough sea tomorrow. What do you
think, Pilot?"

The Navigating Officer nodded:

"Yes, Sir. I reckon it'll blow like this for days. There'll be snow squalls too. Seems as if we're in for some genuine Arctic weather. No place for a married man, Sir."

He pulled the hood of his duffle-coat over his head and thrust his hands deep into its capacious pockets.

Towards noon, when the practice had been duly completed, the Chief-of-Staff invited the Admiral into the chart-house. Important wireless messages had come in and the Admiral and his staff were soon bending over the charts displayed in the warm, brightly lit room. Sir Bruce quickly scanned the reports and measured various distances on the same chart as had been used at the previous day's conference—that of the sea area between Iceland and Bear Island. The wireless messages said that the convoy J.W.55 B had been located by the Luftwaffe and was now being continually shadowed from the air. The Admiral laid his compasses on the chart-table. "Just as I expected," he said, and looked again at that spot on the chart where a lightly pencilled cross marked the position of the convoy.

It was now midday, December 24th. The Admiral deliberated for a few moments. The convoy which he was to cover was at that time steaming between Jan Mayen and Bear Island, somewhat nearer to Jan Mayen.

"This is disquieting," Sir Bruce went on. "If a surface attack should develop now, the convoy would be practically unprotected. Force 1 under Admiral Burnett is not near enough yet and the U-boats will certainly be trailing it."

The Chief-of-Staff, who had also been measuring the current distance between the Force and the convoy, straightened himself:

"German surface forces have never made a sortie to the westward, and I don't think they'll do it now. The convoy is still well to the west of Bear Island."

They conferred for some time, examining possible alternatives and considering whether they would be justified in breaking the W/T silence—maintained during every sortie—to pass an order to the convoy itself. The Admiral's anxiety for the safety of the convoy eventually tipped the scales. Sir Bruce announced his decision:

"I consider it necessary to break W/T silence. Send a wireless message to J.W.55 B at 1400 hours. The convoy is to reduce speed for three hours. And tell the Captain of the *Duke of York* that the Force will proceed at increased speed, say 19 knots. I know this won't bring us much nearer to J.W.55 B, but it may prevent the *Scharnhorst* from coming up on the convoy before dark. Provided of course," the Admiral added, "that she is at sea. Personally I think she is."

The wireless messages went out as ordered. There were no further developments the same day and the original intentions for the covering forces were duly resumed.

# IX

## THE NET IS CAST

TOWARDS evening on December 24th it became apparent that the J.W. convoy, owing no doubt to the drastically worsening weather, was not advancing at the prescribed speed. It further seemed certain that the R.A. convoy coming from Murmansk had already passed Bear Island without having been spotted by the enemy. Once more the Admiral and his staff reviewed the situation in the chart-house. The Admiral, who was checking reports of new positions on the chart, looked up:

"The R.A. convoy has obviously remained undetected. This inclines me all the more to the opinion that our own convoy will be attacked. The U-boats are almost certainly already on its trail. The *Scharnhorst* will come out and attack this convoy. I am more than ever convinced of this."

He paused and remained for a moment deep in thought. Then he gave fresh orders to his Chief-of-Staff:

"Please request Rear-Admiral Destroyers, Home Fleet, to take the following action if possible: first, to divert the R.A. convoy to the north to clear the target area for us. Secondly, to detach four destroyers from convoy R.A.55 A and send them to convoy J.W.55 B. In my opinion the R.A. convoy is now safe but it is quite certain that the Germans will hurl everything they have got at our J.W. convoy."

The Chief-of-Staff took up the pad of W/T blanks

lying at hand, scribbled a few lines, and handed the form to the Signals Officer, who hurried off to have the message coded and transmitted.

"I now feel confident," declared the Admiral, when the door had closed behind the Signals Officer, "that Burnett and his Force 1 with its cruisers and escorting destroyers can drive off the *Scharnhorst* if she should appear, or at any rate inflict such damage as will give us time to close in with Force 2."

At this moment the ship, which for hours had been pursuing her course with an alarming roll, heeled over frantically. Everyone in the chart-house was thrown off balance and groped instinctively for support.

"Terrific seaway," commented Sir Bruce, grasping the firmly anchored chart-table.

"Certainly is, Sir," the Chief-of-Staff concurred, rubbing an elbow which had come into contact with one of the radiators. "A full-scale storm with snow squalls."

December 25th passed without further incident. The gale had now reached its full force, while eddies of snow swept in at intervals from the darkness. During the night of the 25th/26th December, Force 2 steered eastwards at 17 knots. The *Duke of York* was a rigid, unyielding vessel and shipped enormous quantities of water in conditions such as these, although she ran almost before the wind and the sea. Heavy breakers piled up against her upright stem, remained for seconds aloft like shimmering towers of pallid foam, and then thundered their tons of icy Arctic water over the long forecastle, the quadruple turret and the twin turret above it, and, rebounding from the turret armour, shot torn sheets of salty spray to the bridge above. The side-decks and the quarter-deck were likewise engulfed in masses of water. Conditions became more difficult as the heavy ship staggered about in the rough sea like a drunken man. Few of her crew got any sleep during that night of storm—the same night on which the *Scharnhorst* and her five destroyers left Alta Fjord.

At 0339 hours on December 26th the Signals Officer of Force 2 entered the Admiral's quarters on the bridge. He hesitated for one moment as he observed that Sir Bruce, in spite of the heavy roll, had fallen asleep in one of the heavy fixed chairs.

"A wireless message from the Admiralty, Sir!"

The Admiral, wide awake in an instant, leaped to his feet and reached for the message.

"The Chief-of-Staff has already been informed, Sir," reported the Signals Officer, noting with pleasure that the Admiral smiled as he read the message. There was a knock on the door and the Chief-of-Staff entered and reported.

"There you are," exclaimed the Admiral triumphantly. "Just as I predicted! They surmise at the Admiralty that the *Scharnhorst* is at sea. When was the signal sent? Let's see—Aha! It's timed 0319 hours. Come along, gentlemen!"

Sir Bruce hurried to the door, moving expertly to counterbalance the frantic rolling of the ship, and, followed by the other two, led the way through the narrow passage to the chart-house. All three were soon bending over the charts.

"If the *Scharnhorst* attacks in daylight, that is to say during the noon twilight, and immediately retires, we won't get her, Sir," said the Chief-of-Staff.

"No, unfortunately not," agreed the Admiral and placed his hand heavily on the chart. "We aren't close enough yet to cut off her retreat."

"Excuse me, Sir," interjected the Signals Officer, "but we certainly *shall* get her. Force 1 will catch her and stop her."

"God willing," murmured Sir Bruce. Then he turned to his Chief-of-Staff·

"When will the destroyers from R.A.55 A reach our J.W. convoy?"

"Four o'clock tonight at the latest, Sir."

"What ships have been detached?"

The Chief-of-Staff took a slip of paper from his breast pocket:

"*Musketeer, Opportune, Virago* and *Matchless*, Sir. The Rear-Admiral, Destroyers, reported them."

"Good. That means four new big types. Excellent. Meanwhile we know that U-boats are still tailing the convoy. We've no need to worry any more about that R.A. convoy. It is already out of danger. But our J.W. . . ."

The Admiral knitted his brows. Once again he bent over the chart, checking the distances and the positions of the single forces and convoys.

"The J.W. convoy," Sir Bruce went on, "is now at the same longitude and to the south of Bear Island. Right in the danger zone. True, if we again break W/T silence we shall betray the presence of covering forces, but the safeguarding of the convoy is of paramount importance and must be our first consideration. Therefore my orders are that the convoy shall be diverted to the north."

Sir Bruce lowered his voice:

"Perhaps it will then be more difficult for the *Scharnhorst* to find it. On account of the change of course."

Again the Admiral paused. Then he resumed in a tone of authority:

"Secondly: Force 1, that is the 10th Cruiser Squadron, shall report its position immediately. The 17th Destroyer Flotilla supporting the convoy shall likewise report the position of the convoy. Is that clear?"

"Aye, aye, Sir," said the Chief-of-Staff, making rapid notes.

"Thirdly: Inform all of our own position, course and speed. That's all for the time being. Time?"

The Signals Officer glanced at his watch.

"0410 hours, Sir."

The wireless messages were accordingly transmitted and in due course answered by Force 1 and the 17th Destroyer Flotilla.

Outside the storm was in full fury, and the heavy seas were creating great difficulties for the destroyers which were running before the wind. They rolled and pitched and were thrown off course this way and that. Practically submerged in foam and spray, it looked at times as if they must be turned broadside and capsize. Even the long bows of the *Duke of York* were continually awash. The white-flecked sea roared over the breakwater and across any other obstacle it met right up to the lower edge of the 14-inch quadruple turret. The heavy battleship was turning up the sea like a giant snow-plough.

At 0628 hours Sir Bruce had the convoy change course to 45° and ordered Force 1 to close the convoy for mutual support. It was his wish that the cruiser squadron should have destroyers near at hand. At 0712 hours Force 1 again changed course to 270°, in order to close the convoy from the south and, in case of an encounter, to avoid having to steam at full speed against the storm and a rough sea running from the south-west. When, at 0815 hours, Vice-Admiral Burnett received from the 17th Destroyer Flotilla the position, course and speed of the convoy, he changed the course of his cruisers *Belfast*, *Norfolk* and *Sheffield* to 305° and proceeded at a speed of 24 knots.

The net which was to entangle the *Scharnhorst* had not yet been closed, but it had been cast.

# X

## THE *SCHARNHORST* ON HER SORTIE

DURING the night of December 25th/26th the *Scharnhorst* proceeded on her sortie with the five escorting destroyers. Set on a northerly course, blacked-out, with war-watches closed up at action stations, the battleship rolled on before the south-westerly gale. Slowly the Radar beams scanned the darkness, while look-outs on the bridges, control positions, searchlights and guns scrutinized their allotted sectors.

Sailing before the wind with the gently swaying motion and rhythmical pitching characteristic of the long ship, the *Scharnhorst* was spared the worst effects of the gale blowing from astern. But snow squalls impeded visibility, the sky was as dark as the sea, and the escorting destroyers were hardly discernible. From time to time a breaker reared up before the battleship, stood for seconds in a column of pale foam, then collapsed over the bows and ebbed away before the breakwater in gurgling eddies. Smaller breakers, churned up to left and right by the great curving bows, disintegrated in white pennants. The night was icy cold. Cold, too, were the lashes of salty spray which flung themselves across the armour of the forward triple turrets and whipped up to the bridge.

The dense snow and quickly forming ice obscured the lenses of range-finders and directors, rendering them practically useless, and the vigilance of the bridge and signal watches, the look-outs on deck, at the search-light control columns and at the guns was therefore of vital importance. Important too was the Radar appara-tus. Although the two Radar-sets fitted in the *Scharn-horst* were capable of detecting the approach of enemy units within a limited range, they could not—as the British "Rotterdam-apparatus" could—register and make visible the outline and size of any ship so located. However, the Captain, squatting on the little emer-gency seat next to the Officer-of-the-Watch, his broad frame wrapped in a sheepskin coat and a thick scarf wound several times round his neck, knew that he could depend on his look-outs. They always had been first-class in German warships. Furthermore, the men had recently been issued with the new T-glasses that gave excellent definition even by night.

From the bridge nothing could be seen through the driving snow. When the snow flurries abated for a while as though gathering strength for their next on-slaught, huge dark waves loomed in sight, rolling along-side, blue-black, white-crested, thundering against the ship's sides. The breakers, coming at long intervals, rushed across the forecastle with deafening roar, shrouded the long bows in a veil of swirling foam, swept across the anchor chains and, as the bows rose, drained away through the scuppers.

Little was to be heard above the roar of the sea and the intermittent howling of the gale. Here, a water-tight door would bang; there, the clatter of heavy boots on wooden gratings could be heard as one of the watches on the bridge stamped to keep his feet warm. The soft regular hum of the electrical generating plant spread its soothing sound through the stillness of the control positions and turrets. Otherwise there was silence. Every man was tense with expectancy. Any moment the alarm might sound and the ship that was

gliding so smoothly ahead would be suddenly trans-
formed, as if ignited, into a volcano belching fire.

Meanwhile further wireless messages were being
exchanged.

While the Battle Group was still passing through the
outer barrage and steering through Stjern Sund,
Stoeroey Sund and Lappahavet towards the open sea, a
wireless message from the Commodore of U-boats went
out to the eight U-boats that were operating astride the
convoy's route. At 1952 hours the U-boats were ordered
to seize any opportunity that presented itself to launch
torpedoes, notwithstanding the high seaway. Shortly
after this order had been received the U-boat of Oberleutnant zur See Dunkelberg reported that a torpedo
fired from her stern had just missed a destroyer and
that after submerging she had been passed by the
convoy.

At about 2100 hours the Air Officer Commanding
Lofoten reported that the day's reconnaissance by
Radar aircraft had failed to locate either the convoy
or its covering forces. The Luftwaffe had lost contact
with the convoy.

At 2340 hours, three-quarters of an hour after the
Battle Group had passed Point Lucie, one of the
*Scharnhorst's* Signals Officers appeared on the bridge.
He came straight from the bright light of the action
control room, and it took him a little time to get used
to the darkness of the steering-position.

"Where's the Captain?"

"Forrard, with the O.O.W." a voice replied from
out of the darkness, while a guiding hand grasped the
officer's arm and guided him to the Captain.

"Two wireless messages, Herr Kapitän; one of them
from the Grand-Admiral."

"Well, well," said the Captain, always ready to see
the humorous side, "shouldn't the lion be in his bunk

at this time? Let's see what the Grand-Admiral has to say."

He switched on his blue-screened torch and read the message.

"Right; I'll tell the men later. Who's the other message from?"

"From the Commodore of U-boats to Flotilla Eisenbart, Herr Kapitän."

The Sub-Lieutenant handed the other messageform to the Captain. Once more the torch flashed on. The message was timed 2330 hours and contained an order for the eight U-boats to undertake a patrol sweep within certain squares (on the squared chart) if contact with the convoy was lost and no reliable indication as to its whereabouts was available. The Captain nodded:

"Thank you!"

The Grand-Admiral's radio message ran as follows:

(a) Important enemy convoy carrying food and war material to the Russians further imperils our heroic Army on the Eastern Front. We must help.

(b) Attack convoy with *Scharnhorst* and destroyers.

(c) Exploit tactical situation with skill and daring. Do not end the engagement with a partial success. Go all out and see the job right through. Best chance of success lies in superior firingpower of *Scharnhorst*, therefore try to bring her into action. Deploy destroyers accordingly.

(d) Break off according to your own judgment. Break off in any circumstances if faced by heavy units.

(e) Inform crews accordingly. I have every confidence in you.

*Heil und Sieg*
DÖNITZ, Grossadmiral.

The Captain leant on the guard-rail, considering

how he should pass the Grand-Admiral's message on to the men. He would make the announcement himself the following morning at the change-over of the war-watches, i.e. at 0400 hours or shortly before when the previous watch was still on duty and the next one was being mustered on the lower deck.

During the first hour of December 26th, between midnight and one o'clock, more wireless messages came in, again from the Air Officer Commanding Lofoten. The first, arriving at 0028 hours, reported that an air-craft had shadowed the convoy on the previous day, the 25th, from 1343 hours to 1625 hours. The aircraft had maintained contact with the widely spaced column. The second report, which came in at 0051 hours, said that a flying-boat of the type BV 138 had also made contact with the convoy from 1225 hours to 1510 hours on the same day. Neither aircraft had been able to determine the exact composition of the convoy, but the flying-boat had been able to establish that there were no covering forces detached from the convoy within a radius of fifty miles. This information had been obtained by Radar. Unfortunately neither report gave positions.

Captain Hintze scrutinized both wireless messages with care. He was indignant.

"How is it possible," he said, "that this important information has only just come in? The reconnaissance aircraft made contact yesterday afternoon, and now," he glanced at his watch, "we get the information one hour after midnight. Can you understand it?"

The Signals Officer who had brought the messages to the bridge took the forms back again:

"No, Herr Kapitän, it's quite incomprehensible. Between the sortie and the arrival of the messages there's a lapse of more than twelve hours. *And* no positions given!"

"Has there been any reply from Naval Command to our signal concerning the destroyers?" asked the Captain. "The one that the C.-in-C. had transmitted around midnight?"

"No, Herr Kapitän. I will report immediately if anything comes through."

The Captain was referring to the wireless signal which Rear-Admiral Bey had sent to Group North/Navy at 2355 hours:

"In operation area probably SW 6–8; firing-power of destroyers seriously impaired. Speed reduced."

The Commander-in-Chief had apparently had doubts about the operational efficiency of the 4th Destroyer Flotilla and had sent the signal without first securing an appreciation of the weather situation from the leader of the flotilla, Captain Johannesson. The remarkable thing was that the signal had broken the W/T silence usually maintained during an operation, or more precisely, during a sortie for an impending operation, and it seemed possible that the British located this wireless signal and were thereby able to ascertain the position of the *Scharnhorst*.

In any event within three hours of the dispatch of the *Scharnhorst's* signal, the Admiralty informed the British Commander-in-Chief, Admiral Fraser, that they assumed the *Scharnhorst* was at sea. It is also possible, of course, that the Admiralty had the information from Norwegian partisans.

The reply of Group North/Navy to the Commander-in-Chief's wireless message was received in the *Scharnhorst* at about 0300 hours:

"If destroyers cannot keep sea, possibility of *Scharnhorst* completing task alone using mercantile warfare tactics should be considered. Decision rests with Admiral commanding."

The Admiral was now moved to take the opinion of

the leader of the Destroyer Flotilla on the weather situation. This was transmitted to the *Scharnhorst* by visual signals:

"Following sea and wind. No difficulties so far, but situation remains problematical. Expect weather to improve."

Half an hour later, at 0327 hours, U-boat Dunkelberg reported:

"Square AB 6642 forced to submerge by covering forces. South 7, sea 6–7, visibility 1,600 yards."

On receiving this message Captain Hintze went down to the chart-house to consult the squared chart. The Navigating Officer, Korvettenkapitän Lanz, was just plotting the reported position of the convoy. He indicated the point:

"Here, Sir. I plotted the course of the convoy from earlier reports and the report just in confirms it exactly."

Satisfied, the Captain left the chart-house and returned to his seat on the bridge.

At 0345 hours Captain Hintze stretched his frozen limbs and with the assurance born of long experience of big ships and rough seas—legs wide apart, toes pointing in a little, pliant knees to balance every movement—walked over to the steering position. He entered the lower conning-tower through the small door and edged his way between men and apparatus to the Officer-of-the-Watch.

Ordinary Seaman First Class, Günter Sträter, loading number at the IV port 5·9-inch gun—one of the few who survived that day—gave a start as the Captain's voice, coming over the ship's broadcasting system, called the men to attention:

"Captain to all stations. Wireless message from the Grand-Admiral: Seize on the convoy whenever and wherever you get the chance. You will be relieving the Eastern Front. Dönitz, Grossadmiral."

G

The men looked at each other, confident, smiling:
"Sure! We'll get it!"

Then silence fell once more.

At 0400 hours the men who had been keeping constant watch from the bridges, look-outs and guns were relieved from below and were able to take some rest, close to their action stations, where they lay fully clothed on hammocks or blankets securely slung. But sleep came to only a few. They knew that some time during the coming morning they would run into the convoy, always assuming, of course, that the U-boat and aircraft reports were accurate and that the position of the convoy had been correctly estimated by the Admiral's staff. But they were confident that the Admiral, known to them for so long as Commodore of Destroyers, would seek out the convoy. No one aboard the *Scharnhorst* had any doubts about that.

At this time the *Scharnhorst* and her destroyers were about 114 miles south-west of Bear Island. At 0423 hours the Commander-in-Chief had the Battle Group change course to 30° and after another half-hour he turned it back to 4°. Rear-Admiral Bey, who was himself at the chart-table comparing the convoy's reported position and his own, looked at the Captain:

"If the convoy continues on the assumed course and we maintain our present course, we should at 0630 be within about 30 miles."

Captain Hintze agreed. "The only trouble is that visibility is deteriorating all the time," he added.

The Admiral shrugged his shoulders:

"That can't be helped, but I imagine our Radar will pick it up when we get that far."

He turned back to the chart, worked with course triangles, compasses and pencil for a while, then scribbled a few lines on a W/T blank and handed it to the Signals Officer:

"Put this through by R/T to Z 29 at 0700 hours!"

It was an order for the 4th Destroyer Flotilla to deploy at 0700 hours into a reconnaissance sweep astride the assumed approach of the convoy, each ship to be routed singly, speed 10 knots, course 250°. The *Scharnhorst* was to remain roughly ten miles behind the destroyer line. Shortly afterwards the destroyers took up their new positions as ordered. One hour later, at 0755 hours, Rear-Admiral Bey ordered the destroyers by wireless signal to alter course to 230°. At about 0730—according to the account of the survivors—the loudspeaker system had blared through the ship:

"Clear ship for action. Sound action stations."

This meant that the enemy must be in the vicinity and might be sighted at any moment. It also meant that no longer only half the crew, one war-watch, but the entire crew were closed up at the guns, standing by at boilers and engines, and manning all positions for navigation and fire-control—in short that every man of the 1,900 who formed the ship's complement was ready for action. Reports from all stations converged at the control position until the First Officer, Fregatten-kapitän Dominik, was able to report "ship clear for action" to the Captain. He in turn passed the report to the Admiral. Shortly afterwards an announcement for the crew came through the loudspeakers:

"Our destroyers are advancing to the westward for reconnaissance."

Everyone knew now that the five big destroyers of the 4th Flotilla, each of nearly 2,000 tons, were spread out into their reconnaissance sweep, scouring the sea like a huge rake, searching for their prey. The *Scharnhorst* was following.

It was tough going for the destroyers. On their new course they had to head right into the teeth of the gale. They laboured in the high seas which were coming over from SW with force 6. The sharp wedges of their bows ploughed up mountains of water and they were enveloped from stem to stern in cascades of foam which covered everything on deck almost instantaneously with a sheet of solid ice. Dense squalls of snow whipped cruelly into the numbed faces of bridge watches and gun crews, encrusting hair and brows with ice, freezing features into wooden stiffness, blotting out all visibility. The night-glasses were useless. The crews of the 5-inch and 5.9-inch guns, although strapped fast by ropes with swivel hooks, could hardly keep their feet as the ships jerked and pitched and pounded. The few who were obliged for one reason or another to pass along deck had to fight their way through, clutching the ridge ropes, in constant danger of being washed overboard. Between pitching movements the destroyers were heeling over alarmingly; only those with single mountings instead of twin turrets on their forecastles were able to ride the heavy sea with comparative safety.

The *Scharnhorst* herself after approximately one hour, that is at about 0820 hours, adopted a more northerly course. No report of this change of course reached the destroyers, and they therefore maintained their own course more to the westward. At the same time, between 0822 and 0935 hours, the leader of the Destroyer Flotilla transmitted a reconnaissance signal to the Commander-in-Chief which subsequently had to be corrected. This is what happened:

Z 29, the leading destroyer, sighted by Radar and shortly afterwards also visually, a vessel on the starboard bow steering a parallel course at a distance of 30 cables. Z 30, stationed on the starboard beam of the leading destroyer, also reported the vessel and assumed it to be an enemy ship. At 0935 hours the ship, which was visible merely as a vague silhouette, was challenged and replied with the correct recognition signal. The flotilla now realized that it was one of their own destroyers, Z 38, which on taking up her position in the reconnaissance sweep had got on to the wrong course, too far to the northward. Z 38 now reverted speedily to her correct position and the flotilla leader, Captain Johannesson, corrected his previous signal to the Commander-in-Chief.

In the midst of the excitement caused by this confusion the destroyers sighted starshell about twelve miles astern. The shooting of starshell, which in the Arctic twilight looked like the appearance and disappearance of many golden-yellow suns between sea and sky, lasted from 0920 hours to 0930 hours. Aboard the destroyers they felt sure that the fire lay above the *Scharnhorst* and that it could only mean that the enemy had located the battleship. Half an hour later they picked up a wireless message from the *Scharnhorst* which said:

"Square AC 4133 under fire from enemy cruisers!"

The position given in this signal aroused consternation in Z 29, for according to it the *Scharnhorst* must have been standing, not the agreed 10 miles, but 50 miles to the eastward of the destroyers. Later investigations suggested that an error had occurred either in transmitting or reading the Commander-in-Chief's signal and that instead of the number 4199 on the squared chart—as would probably have been written in the original message—4133 was substituted.

On board the *Scharnhorst* the message from the flotilla leader erroneously reporting that an enemy destroyer had been sighted, caused Captain Hintze to announce to all stations:

"Wireless message from the destroyers: Destroyers are in action!"

Although this announcement had eventually to be contradicted—and such errors of judgment are always

possible in conditions of darkness and driving snow—
it had an electrifying effect on all who heard it. The
look-outs redoubled their vigilance and everyone hoped
that the next few minutes would bring an encounter
with enemy forces, perhaps even with the convoy itself.

And this, indeed, is what happened—but in a way
very different from that which anyone on board
expected.

# XI

## VICE-ADMIRAL BURNETT ATTACKS WITH THE 10TH CRUISER SQUADRON, FORCE 1

D URING the whole of December 26th Acting Chief Petty Officer Willi Gödde stood at his port forward searchlight-control column on look-out duty. These installations, known to the ratings, not quite correctly, as "director columns", were fitted on either side of the bridge somewhat abaft the armoured fire-control position, and were used for look-out duty because of their outstanding optical performance. P.O. Gödde, a quiet, serious type of man with religious leanings, could not be relieved all day because the Petty Officer who usually took over from him, a trainer in "B" turret, was away on leave.

Gödde was wearing his telephone apparatus slung round his neck and so was in constant communication with the ship's command. He was able to listen to everything that was discussed at the control position and follow the entire sequence of events.

Suddenly at 0920 hours huge columns of water, nine feet in diameter, spurted up out of the darkness about 500 yards abeam of the control column. Phantom-like in their pale unreality they were clearly visible through the drifting snow.

"Shell splashes", darted through the P.O.'s mind. "Eight-inch shells at least." He turned the speaking-switch of his telephone . . .

And then everything happened at once.

The forward Radar reported the enemy. Alarm bells rang. Gödde heard a confusion of voices; directors on all stations picking up the target; orders, commands. Then the barrels of the after "C" turret began to thunder.

An action had started, but not against the convoy and its cargo ships; warships had opened fire on the *Scharnhorst*.

A far-off angry rumbling snarled across the sea and the night was lit with flashes of fire. On the port quarter, on a bearing of 245°, orange-red flames burst out of the darkness. Gödde could see quite clearly the snowflakes dancing in the fiery light, and shortly after the German guns had fired their second salvo he heard the answering roar of the enemy's guns. Then he was momentarily dazzled by the long sheets of flame which burst from the *Scharnhorst's* own armament, while the ship was wrapped in a cloud of warm acrid fumes. Gödde pressed his eyes hard against the rubber-cushioned lenses of his apparatus, but in vain; he could see no more than the enemy's gunflashes; of the ship that was firing he could see nothing. Perhaps there were two ships, perhaps three—he could not tell. But one thing was certain: the ship that was hidden there, sending over salvo after salvo, must be a heavy cruiser with 8-inch armament.

Starshell was also being fired, obviously from another ship, to allow the heavy cruiser to observe the fall of shot around her target, the *Scharnhorst*.

The action lasted fifteen minutes, that is until 0940 hours. It was impossible to say whether any hits had been scored on the enemy. Shortly after opening fire the *Scharnhorst* altered course to 150°, almost a complete turn round, and increased her speed to 30 knots. Her task was to annihilate the convoy. To engage in battle with enemy cruisers that were certainly armed with torpedoes, in the pitch darkness—dawn would not begin to break until 11 a.m.—was certainly no part of her duty. The German Commander-in-Chief could now assume that the cruisers were standing to the southward of the convoy and that he would certainly have come upon the convoy itself had not the cruisers fallen upon the *Scharnhorst* like angry watch-dogs. The convoy could not be far off now, it must be steaming somewhere to the north of the cruiser line, and as the speed of the *Scharnhorst* was thought to be superior to that of her opponents, she could easily disengage, try to work round the cruisers and attack the convoy from a different direction.

The *Scharnhorst* did not, however, emerge from this encounter unscathed. A report reached the forward fire-control position from the port III 5·9 gun:

"Hit between port III gun and torpedo-tubes. Shell has not exploded."

Ordinary Seaman First Class Sträter serving in the IV 5·9 turret heard later that this shell had penetrated the upper deck, and come to rest in compartment IX, the office of the technical P.O.s in the forward crew space of the 4th Division. The gun crew had only just been apprised of this when the Signals-Transmitter turned the talking-switch of his telephone and raised his hand:

"Attention! The foretop Radar is out of action. A direct hit in the foretop. Casualties among the A.A. crew."

As a result of the same hit, splinters were falling, fortunately without causing further damage, on to the small open platform where P.O. Gödde stood at his control column. Through his earphones he too heard the reports of the two hits. He learned also that fire had broken out on the lower deck when the unexploded shell had come through, but that it was quickly got under control.

While the *Scharnhorst* was disengaging the Captain ordered a smoke-screen, and as the ship sped away at 30 knots great clouds of dense white smoke formed a solid wall behind her. Then the loudspeaker was heard again:

"Lull in action. We are trying once more to get at the convoy, the destroyers from the south, we in the *Scharnhorst* from the north."

This information had a tonic effect on every man on board. It had been foul luck running into those cruisers instead of the convoy, but they'd shake them off! They wouldn't be beaten. Just give them a chance to get at 'em!

During the lull, Staff Chief-Gunner Wibbelhoff and the Chief Gunners of the other turrets were ordered to report to the Gunnery Commander on the bridge. Wibbelhoff, a warrant officer with more than fifteen years of service behind him, was responsible for training the port 5·9-inch battery and was posted in the port IV 5·9-inch twin turret next to Chief Gunner C.P.O. Moritz. It was some time before he returned. His gun-crew looked at him expectantly. He was an affable type and was on the best of terms with his men. He gave a quick gesture with his right hand:

"Well, boys, the forrard Radar has had it!"

The men refused to be dismayed.

"Oh, that old mattress! Anyway there's still one aft!"

All the same the news had shaken them. The older men with experience of the Atlantic operation knew the value of Radar only too well. They also knew that the *Scharnhorst*, more than any other warship, always got the newest gadgets and that gunnery practice had been carried out with Radar control.

"I don't like it." The Chief Gunner was not so sanguine. "It's like being blind in one eye.... Ah, well, we'll probably get by with the after Radar."

They had no idea that British Radar had meanwhile been developed to such a pitch that it turned night into day and that after the loss of the forward Radar they were in the position of a blind man fighting an all-seeing opponent; they did not realize that the British could observe their every movement and that neither darkness, snowstorm nor smoke-screen could afford the slightest cover.

It has never been established whether it was the mirror of the foretop Radar which was hit or whether the defect occurred in the transmitting or receiving installations.

The sequence of events during the first encounter between the *Scharnhorst* and the cruisers of Force 1 were, from the British point of view, as follows:

At 0840 hours the Radar in the *Belfast*, Admiral Burnett's flagship, picked up the *Scharnhorst* at a range of 35,000 yards. At this time Force 1 (10th Cruiser Squadron) was heading for the convoy which was still 48 miles distant to the north. The *Scharnhorst* was at this time 36 miles away from the convoy. From 0900 to 0930 hours the British Radar recorded a second echo. It was assumed that this was either one of the merchant ships in the convoy or possibly an enemy destroyer seeking to approach the convoy. As the cruisers intended to attack the *Scharnhorst*, the echo was ignored as being of only secondary importance. Vice-Admiral Burnett therefore kept course in the direction of the German battleship. At 0924 hours the *Belfast* opened fire with starshell and five minutes later Force 1 was ordered to engage with main armament. The *Norfolk*, the only cruiser with 8-inch guns, opened fire with her four twin-turrets at a range of 9,800 yards. She continued firing until 0940 hours. Upon firing the second and third salvoes the British observed that the *Scharnhorst* had been hit. The *Belfast* and *Sheffield* did not participate in the direct firing.

When the *Scharnhorst* retreated and the range opened, the *Norfolk* ceased firing and the squadron pursued the German battleship to the southward. When, at 0955, the *Scharnhorst* turned on to a north-easterly course, the Admiral appreciated at once that she was trying to work round to the northward of the convoy and attack again. As the *Scharnhorst's* speed was estimated at 30 knots and Force I could steam at a maximum speed of only 24 knots in the prevailing gale and sea, Admiral Burnett decided to take a short cut and interpose his force between the convoy and the *Scharnhorst*. He knew that the cruisers' Radar could sight and report the enemy in good time. He had the cruisers alter course accordingly so that at 1020 hours contact with the *Scharnhorst* was lost. The last Radar echo was obtained from the *Scharnhorst* at 36,000 yards when she was steering to the north-east.

During this engagement the British Commander-in-Chief had turned the convoy to the northward for one hour. After contact with the *Scharnhorst* was lost he turned it back to 45°. Half an hour earlier, at 0951 hours, the four destroyers *Musketeer*, *Matchless*, *Opportune* and *Virago* were transferred from the convoy to the cruiser squadron. From the reception of unidentified Radar echoes throughout the engagement, the British Commander-in-Chief assumed that enemy destroyers were in the vicinity.

With the loss of contact with the *Scharnhorst* the first encounter, prelude to the action of December 26th, came to an end.

# XII

## THE SECOND ENCOUNTER WITH FORCE 1

THE *Scharnhorst*, concealed by her smoke-screen, had disappeared on a southerly course. As contact with the British cruisers appeared to have been broken, Rear-Admiral Bey gradually altered course to the northward. His plan of action had been well considered. The battleship's superior speed should allow her to turn the enemy's flank and take him completely by surprise. The one thing which the Commander-in-Chief and his Staff had not reckoned with was the great range and—as was later explicitly acknowledged by the British Commander-in-Chief in his despatch—the outstanding performance of the British "Rotterdam apparatus".

At 1000 hours one of the U-boats, that under Kapitänleutnant Lübsen, again reported the position of the convoy:

"Convoy 0945 hours, square AB 6365."

This meant that the convoy was steaming about 40 miles to the north-west of the German destroyers.

Nine minutes later Rear-Admiral Bey ordered the 4th Destroyer Flotilla to report on the situation.

Z 29 signalled in reply:

"Proceeding according to plan, square AC 4413, course 230°, speed 12 knots."

At 1025 hours the U-boat Lübsen again reported:

"Encountered convoy 0930 hours. Position uncertain."

This report caused the flotilla leader, Captain Johannesson, to consider whether he should carry on with the reconnaissance sweep as ordered by the Commander-in-Chief or attack the convoy independently. His uncertainty was ended by a wireless order of Rear-Admiral Bey received at 1027 hours:

"Fourth Destroyer Flotilla course 70°, speed 25 knots!"

Half an hour later a fresh inquiry from the Commander-in-Chief requested position, course and speed of the flotilla. The reports made by the destroyers to the flotilla leader showed that the flotilla was deployed over a distance of about 30 miles and was correctly stationed for the reconnaissance sweep.

The flotilla leader's expectations of an improvement in the weather had unfortunately not materialized. Visibility had deteriorated and low cloud strata, driven along by the south-westerly gale, obscured the Arctic dawn which was now due. At 1135 hours the *Scharnhorst* ordered a further change of course to 30°, and at 1120 hours indicated her own position according to the squared chart, course 0°, speed 27 knots. This meant that the battleship was now about 50 miles north-east of the destroyers and was steering a northerly course. At 1158 hours Rear-Admiral Bey sent a wireless signal to the destroyers:

"Operate against square 6365!"

The effect of this order was to give the destroyer flotilla the word to attack the convoy according to its last position as given by U-boat Lübsen.

After receiving this order, Captain Johannesson at 1217 hours turned Z 29 on to a course of 280° and increased speed. All the other destroyers were ordered by visual or wireless signal to rally to the destroyer leader for the attack. At 1226 hours the U-boat Commodore, after picking up these various signals and messages, instructed U-boat Lübsen, which had last reported the convoy's position at 0945 hours, to send out D/F signals until 1300 hours. It so happened, however, that in spite of renewed reminders from Z 29, none of these D/F signals was picked up by the destroyers.

The black Arctic night at last yielded to a faint grey dawn. Gale, sea and snow squalls increased. The *Scharnhorst* men remained closed up to action stations, the Commander-in-Chief was on the bridge. With the collar of his heavy sheepskin coat turned up and the big Zeiss night-glasses hanging on their leather slings round his neck, Rear-Admiral Bey gazed into the dancing snow flurries. Next to him stood the Captain, hands encased in fur-lined gloves and thrust deep into his pockets. Korvettenkapitän Bredenbreuker, the Gunnery Commander, in company with his Chief Signals-Transmitter, stepped from his control position on to the bridge. In such thick weather more could be seen from outside than through the lenses of the directors and gun-sights. The Gunnery Signals-Transmitter, an able seaman of long service, leaned nonchalantly against the armoured walls of the control position. He had put on his head-phones and the telephone cable coiled like a thin black snake at his feet. With the sea on her quarter, the ship rolled with a smooth and gentle rhythm. Shortly after 1100 hours, the Navigating Officer appeared on the bridge with a wireless message. It was now sufficiently light for him immediately to recognize the Captain's broad-shouldered figure and he made his way straight to him:

"Report from a reconnaissance aircraft, Sir."

Captain Hintze freed his right hand from his pocket and took the wireless message.

"Splendid. It's remarkable how these chaps manage to keep it up in this foul weather!"

He read the text, frowned and turned to the Commander-in-Chief:

"Not too pleasant, Herr Admiral. But it need not worry us for the time being."

The Admiral took the message form. The report was disquieting. Five units had been sighted far to the north-westward of North Cape, approximately 150 miles to the westward of the *Scharnhorst*. The Commander-in-Chief looked at the Captain with half-closed eyes:

"We'd better make sure exactly where it is. Come along."

They went down to the chart-house together. The Navigating Officer, Korvettenkapitän Lanz, had already plotted the position on the chart. He indicated it with his pencil:

"Here, Herr Admiral."

Rear-Admiral Bey considered for a while:

"In my opinion," he said, "it can only be an enemy Battle Group. One or more heavy units with the usual screen. Or just one heavy unit."

He was silent and the others waited for him to elaborate. The Captain nodded and the Admiral continued:

"Every unit of the convoy's covering force is here in the vicinity. This we have already observed. A second convoy is out of the question. A convoy would never run so close to the Norwegian coast. Apart from that, if the report of only five units is correct the number is far too small for a convoy. We know the position of our own destroyers. Hence it can only be a British Battle Group."

The Commander-in-Chief paused and straightened himself. As former "FdZ", Commodore of Destroyers, he was accustomed to taking quick decisions. One more glance at the chart and his mind was made up. He turned to the Captain:

"In spite of this report we will go ahead with our original intention, Hintze. Maintain course and speed. We'll get at this damned convoy somehow."

The Captain's hand went to the peak of his cap:

"*Jawohl*, Herr Admiral."

The Admiral took a packet of cigarettes from his coat pocket and offered it to the Captain, while Chief-Quartermaster Jürgens—who had been keeping respectfully in the background—stepped forward to offer them a light. Inhaling deeply, the Admiral thanked him and offered the tall, fair Friesian a cigarette. Then, in company with the Captain, he left the chart-house and returned aloft. Back on the bridge, he said:

"The look-out, Hintze, must be first-class. Everything depends on it. Do impress that again on the Gunnery Commander."

Korvettenkapitän Bredenbreuker was listening and motioned to the Admiral that he had understood.

"*Jawohl*, Herr Admiral. The order will be constantly repeated."

He exchanged a few words with his Signals-Transmitter who thereupon turned the switch of his telephone, disentangled with his free hand the long cable coming from the control tower and announced:

"From the Commander-in-Chief to all stations: Intensified look-out!"

According to Karl Peter, author of the book *Schlachtkreuzer Scharnhorst*, Group North/Navy (the authority superior to the Battle Group) had not regarded the five units reported by the reconnaisance aircraft as British ships, but had taken them to be their own German destroyers. They assumed—as indeed happened later—that the Commander-in-Chief had detached them because of the deteriorating weather. Of the origin of the air reconnaissance report Karl Peter

H

relates some interesting details: At a conference held a few weeks later at Tromsoe between officers of the First Battle Group and the Air Officer Commanding North-West, Generalleutnant Roth, it emerged that the observer who, on the morning of December 26th, had spotted the five units, had referred in his report not merely to "five units to the north-west of North Cape", but to "five units, among them probably one heavy unit, to the north-west of North Cape". It remains incomprehensible that the Air Officer Commanding— himself a former naval officer—should have reprimanded the observer on landing, saying that he disliked suppositions in reconnaissance reports and would be obliged if in future the observers would report only what they had actually seen. Incredibly also, the Air Officer had deleted the offending passage referring to the probable presence of one heavy unit when he transmitted the report to Group North/Navy. The position given in the report was also incorrect.

In the *Scharnhorst*, between 1100 and 1130 hours, P.O. Gödde, at the port forward searchlight control column, heard the voice of his Captain. Captain Hintze did not on this occasion use the loudspeaker system, but spoke instead on the artillery telephone:

"From the Captain to all stations: Situation Report. This morning as expected, we ran into the forces covering the convoy—three cruisers of the "town class" type. We have altered course and are now trying to get at the convoy from the other side, that is from the north. We have shaken off the cruisers. An important reconnaissance report has just come in from the Luftwaffe. A British heavy battle group has been sighted 150 miles to the westward; I repeat 150 miles to the westward. That is to say, well out of our way. We are forging on towards the convoy. End of announcement!"

Gödde nodded. He was satisfied. It was very satis-
factory, he thought, how the Captain always took the
men into his confidence, and kept them informed of
the situation. He knew from comrades serving in other
ships that this was not always the case. As a Petty
Officer of long service he knew just how important it
was that the ship's company should be kept informed
of developments during a sortie as far as this was
humanly possible. It helped to keep the men alert and
interested. Every man acknowledged a personal respon-
sibility for the success of the task in hand the moment
he realized that his superiors were treating him not
merely as a recipient of orders, but as a comrade in
arms, and a comrade who in an emergency might have
to step into the place of an officer and had therefore to
be kept in the picture. Every bulletin stimulated the
men's imagination, called forth their co-operation and
increased their self-confidence. A rating who was aware
of the situation on the enemy side, of the distribution
of the forces on his own side, who understood the
Commander-in-Chief's intentions and the meaning of
each new move, would, whether his duty was as a look-
out, with a gun crew or in the W/T office, act and feel
quite differently from a man who was treated merely
as a cog in a great machine. He would grasp the meaning of every new order far better and execute it more
readily. In the *Scharnhorst* the practice of keeping the
men informed was observed by all commanders during
all war cruises and engagements.

About two hours after the first engagement of that
day, Gödde heard contact with the enemy again reported by the after Radar. Soon the alarm bells were
sounding their shrill warning through all decks.

Gödde applied himself to his apparatus with redoubled concentration; carefully he scanned the way
ahead.

At 1221 hours Gödde thought he saw a patch of darkness against the midday twilight on the port and starboard bows. Soon afterwards this became definite shadows. Turning the wheel of his director apparatus with his right hand, he felt for the talking-switch with his left and pushed it over:

"Port and starboard ahead three shadows!"

At the same time Gödde was able to hear how similar reports were coming in at the control position from other stations. As the initial orders went out to the heavy guns, and the directors in the control tower picked up the target, flashes of fire came from the distant shadowy forms, the silhouettes of which were gradually sharpening against the twilight. Once, twice, three times gun flashes broke from the dark shadows that were the enemy ships. Dull explosions above his own ship and the sudden appearance of a yellow glare around him caused Gödde to take his eyes off the targets and look upwards. Three or four dazzling yellow-white suns hovered phantom-like above the *Scharnhorst,* their falling rays starkly illuminating her superstructure and decks. The outlines of the triple turrets and barrels, the bridges and tower roofs rose sharply delineated out of the whirling snow.

"Starshell!" The thought was mechanical, objective. Gödde again glued his eyes to the sights of his apparatus. Great splashes raised steep plumes from the sea close to the ship and at the same moment the two forward 11-inch triple turrets of the *Scharnhorst* opened fire against the enemy ship lying to starboard. The second encounter of December 26th had begun.

Standing in the open on the bridge, Rear-Admiral Bey observed the enemy's fire, while the Captain and Gunnery Commander rushed to their stations in the control position immediately the sighting of British forces was reported. The Admiral then stepped to the port armoured bulkhead of the control position which was still open and shouted his order to the Captain:

"Turn to port; we must get out of this!"

"*Jawohl*, Herr Admiral! Hard a-port! All engines full speed ahead! New course: 135°. To Gunnery Commander: Ship is turning hard a-port."

Quickly increasing her speed, the *Scharnhorst* hauled round on to her easterly course, heeling over heavily to starboard while the fire-control directors of the main and secondary armament held steadily on to their target. In the turrets the gunners followed the pointers to offset the ship's turning. Now the after "C" turret on the quarter-deck could also pick up the target and add the golden-red flames of its triple barrels to the second and third salvoes. Kapitänleutnant Wieting, the Second Gunnery Officer, added the fire of the two forward 5·9-inch twin turrets for as long as they could still reach the target.

P.O. Gödde observed that after the first three or four salvoes from the *Scharnhorst* fire broke out in one of the three British cruisers—the outlines of which were now clearly visible—roughly abreast of her after funnel. Another cruiser was evidently also well ablaze at bows and stern and was giving off a great deal of smoke. Between two salvoes Korvettenkapitän Bredenbreuker announced:

"To all stations: Heavy explosions with the enemy."

Then the heavy guns fired their next salvo. Ahead and astern of the British cruisers the splashes of the 11-inch shells rose mast-high from the sea, stood erect for several seconds like giant fountains and then broke. Broad circles of foam formed in their place and swung up and down with the rhythm of the waves. Gödde noted to his satisfaction that the salvoes which the Gunnery Commander was ordering in quick succession were straddling the enemy almost in every instance.

The *Scharnhorst* kept turning round on to her easterly course and the British cruisers were dropping more and more astern and to port. Once more Gödde, who was keeping his sights trained on the enemy, observed what he thought was a hit in the bows of one of the cruisers. A giant sheet of flame shot from her fore-deck but soon subsided in a cloud of black smoke. It appeared to the P.O. that the enemy's fire, which at first had been well placed, began to falter under the quick-firing salvoes of the *Scharnhorst's* main armament, though the range was much closer than during the first encounter in the morning. After about twenty minutes the enemy was, in the driving snow and rain, completely out of sight.

At 1241 hours the British checked their fire. A quarter of an hour later, at 1300 hours, the Captain transmitted an order to the Gunnery Commander which was thereupon repeated by all Signals Transmitters:

"Lull in action!"

In this action, the second encounter with Force 1 (10th Cruiser Squadron, Admiral Burnett), the *Scharnhorst* was not hit.

Everywhere the gun crews set to work. The brass cartridges of the used ammunition were salvaged or thrown overboard where they had not already been washed away by the heavy seas. The heavy turrets, from which the cordite gases could not always be drawn off quickly enough, were briefly turned into the wind for ventilation. Munition hoists rattled; munition racks were replenished and the ordnance personnel checked consumption in turrets and batteries. Minor damage was quickly repaired by the artificers. Soon the all-clear reports were reaching the Gunnery Commander.

Meanwhile, the Commander-in-Chief was discussing the situation with his staff, the Captain and the Navigating Officer, in the chart-house.

"Damn it," grunted the Admiral, "we're not getting at the convoy at all. The cruisers are always just where we want to strike. They were the same ones as this morning, weren't they, Hintze?"

The Captain pulled the leather cover over the lenses of his big double glasses and remained thoughtful for a moment before replying:

"I'm inclined to agree, Herr Admiral. The AO (Artillery Officer, i.e. Gunnery Commander) thinks so too. It was impossible to see the cruisers this morning, but the shell splashes, which I observed myself, were of the same calibre. The AO thinks they were 8-inch and 5·9-inch shells. I," he added with a smile, "am a torpedo specialist."

"Apparently we're still being shadowed," continued the Rear-Admiral, "according to the after Radar reports at any rate. There's nothing actually to be seen. Let's hope we shake her off in due course. I can see no point in making a third attempt to get at the convoy."

He paused and everyone was silent.

It is not known whether this conference, which doubtless took place after the second engagement, also touched on the superiority of British Radar or on the possible proximity of the heavy enemy units which had been reported at 11 o'clock.

The Admiral went up to the chart-table, checked once more the distance to the north Norwegian coast, glanced at the course and speed indicators and looked at the Captain:

"Return to Norway, Hintze. Alta Fjord. What is the course?"

Korvettenkapitän Lanz, the Navigating Officer, picked up the course triangles, slipped them across the chart, and drew a fine pencil-line:

"One hundred and fifty-five degrees, Herr Admiral."

The Commander-in-Chief nodded to the Captain:

"Course 155° then. Speed 28 knots. You may tell the men that we are returning to base. Thank you, gentlemen."

A few minutes later the *Scharnhorst* slewed round on to her new course. She now had the gale and the sea ahead and to starboard as, her bows washed by the heavy breakers, she pitched southward. The short twilight was already over. Darkness had settled around the ship. She was no longer closed up at action stations, but intensified look-out had been ordered.

It seems probable that Rear-Admiral Bey—possibly concerned by the report that five enemy units had been sighted—chose to make for the Norwegian coast after his second attempt to strike at the convoy had failed, so as not to be cut off by the British Force. From the measures taken by the Commander-in-Chief and from the Captain's words to the crew—as recalled by survivors—one may conclude with reasonable certainty that in the *Scharnhorst* they thought that one of the five units reported was a heavy unit, and the Grand-Admiral's explicit instructions were that the *Scharnhorst* was on no account to enter into an engagement with a heavy unit.

At 1315 hours a wireless report from U-boat Lübsen came through which, timed at 1130 hours, gave a reconnaissance report on the convoy without stating its position.

At 1345 hours, that is to say, after the conclusion of the second encounter with Force 1, the 4th Destroyer Flotilla received an unsigned wireless signal:

"Fourth Destroyer Flotilla break off!"

Upon inquiry from the destroyer leader in Z 30 it was stated that the signature *Scharnhorst* had been transmitted in a garbled form. To Captain Johannesson, leader of the flotilla, the order—quite naturally—

seemed incomprehensible. As it was not clear to him whether it referred to the attack against the convoy as located by U-boat Lübsen, or meant that the entire operation was being called off, he asked the Commander-in-Chief by wireless signal for further instructions. The *Scharnhorst's* reply, received at 1420 hours, was:

"Return to base!"

The reasons which prompted the Commander-in-Chief's decision are not known; no further wireless signals—which might have explained it—were transmitted to the flotilla and none of the *Scharnhorst's* officers, who might have known why the Admiral dismissed the destroyers, survived. Obviously the decision was not influenced by fuel shortage or weather conditions. The British destroyers, which were of similar tonnage, had to face the same difficulties when the seas roughened during the morning, and managed to hold out. Rear-Admiral Bey, as former Commodore of Destroyers, would know better than anyone what he could expect of his destroyers and he was well acquainted with the traditional pugnacity which characterized this arm of the Navy.

The flotilla leader of course obeyed the order and turned on to a southerly course, making for Point Lucie I at a speed of 12 knots.

Subsequent events as affecting the 4th Destroyer Flotilla may be anticipated at this point. On mustering, it was found that Z 33 was missing, and she did not report again until 0030 hours on the following day, December 27th. At 1840 hours a mutilated wireless message timed 1656 hours came through, bringing the first news that the *Scharnhorst* was in action against a British battleship. It is not known why this message did not reach the destroyers until 2 hours and 16 minutes after its transmission. Almost simultaneously they picked up a wireless message from Group North/Navy timed 1736 hours:

"1656 hours reports English unit battleship at 20°; 6 miles off. Course 120°."

This message implied that Admiral Fraser in the *Duke of York* had indicated his position to his forces by wireless at 1656 hours. The monitoring service of Group North/Navy had picked up this signal, and within 40 minutes it was decoded and handed to the wireless telegraphist of Group North/Navy timed 1736 hours for transmission to the Battle Group *Scharnhorst*. An excellent achievement.

While returning to the Norwegian coast the destroyers picked up a wireless message from the *Scharnhorst*. It was timed 1819 hours and must therefore have been sent during the artillery duel between the *Scharnhorst* and the *Duke of York*. It ran:

"Enemy firing with Radar control at a range of more than 19,500 yards."

This message came as a surprise to all departments of the German Navy, demonstrating as it did the considerable superiority of British Radar which until then had been known to only a few specialists in Germany.

At 1911 hours an order from the Commodore of U-boats to the eight boats of Flotilla Eisenbart was overheard:

"Make for square AC 4940 immediately at full speed."

Shortly afterwards Group North/Navy informed the 1st Battle Group:

"U-boats and destroyers have been ordered to battle area at top speed."

Although the 4th Destroyer Flotilla had still received no direct order the flotilla leader decided to make for the battle area at once. Scarcely had he given the appropriate orders and shaped course towards the square indicated by the wireless message from Group North/Navy, than the following order from the Group came in to Z 29:

"Make from the coast for battle area *Scharnhorst*, square AC 4677. Report your position by short-code signal."

The flotilla altered course to 140°, later to 150° in the direction of North Cape and slowly increased speed to 27 knots. Captain Johannesson reported on his position by short-code signal as ordered.

With the sea hitting them almost square abeam the destroyers lurched along their prescribed course. They knew now that the *Scharnhorst* was in action with a British heavy unit and that further British forces were almost certainly participating in the battle—possibly cruisers standing by the heavy unit, the cruisers of the two morning encounters and doubtless a certain number of destroyers. This was a combination for which the *Scharnhorst* was obviously no match. It is clear from the speed ordered by the flotilla leader how determined they were, in spite of the weather, to go to the aid of their comrades engaged in battle. Would they arrive in time? Would they be able to help? On the bridge of every destroyer the same thought predominated, the same determination to get at the enemy at all costs. So they forged doggedly ahead through the darkness, heeling over mightily to either side. The telegraphists waited in vain for further news, for reports from the *Scharnhorst*, but the eerie, portentous silence which surrounded her remained unbroken.

The destroyers had been pursuing their new course for about an hour, when an order from Group North/ Navy timed 2013 hours reached them:

"Break off operation immediately. Avoid contact with enemy. Make at once for the Schären Islands."

The flotilla made at high speed for the coast which was located by Radar at a distance of about 200 miles, at 2330 hours. At 0150 hours on December 27th they entered the Schären through Rolvsbottn and Kval Sund at a speed of 17 knots. At 0350 hours they received a wireless signal from Z 33, which was proceeding on an independent course, that she had passed Point Lucie I at 0120 hours. At about 10 o'clock the 4th Destroyer Flotilla anchored inside Kaa Fjord by the *Tirpitz*. For them the action was over.

To return now to the *Scharnhorst*. At 1430 hours on December 26th the Captain gave a situation report over the telephone system:

"We have just been in action with three cruisers, the same ones as this morning. As many of you will have seen, they have been well and properly hit. The Commander-in-Chief detached the destroyers after our first encounter and sent them home. As the weather is getting steadily worse we are also returning to base and are making now for Norway."

At 1500 hours an order came through the ship's broadcasting system:

"From the First Officer to all stations: Action Messing!"

P.O. Gödde had eaten nothing all day. There was no one to fetch food for him and he could not leave his post. The after Radar was persistently reporting that the *Scharnhorst* was being shadowed by a contact cruiser and the distance of this vessel was being given from time to time. Gödde was a man of initiative and he was anxious to know how the operation was working out. Eventually hunger prevailed, however, and he spoke to the control position on his portable telephone:

"P.O. Gödde, port forward searchlight-control column, requests to be relieved for a few minutes to get food."

He heard his request passed on; then came the voice of Signals-Transmitter:

"Relief coming up at once. Message from the Gunnery Officer: Go to the galley as quickly as possible."

Gödde was duly relieved and hurried off, slipping badly on the icy deck of the labouring ship. In the galley he met about fifteen comrades, late-comers like himself, discussing the general situation. Some of them appeared not to have heard the Captain's announcement. One turned to Gödde and said: "Do you know what's happening? Why are we turning back?"

Gödde had a strange, uneasy feeling. It seemed to him that there was something threatening in the air. Was this a premonition of what was to come? He did not know, but felt only that he must return to his action station as quickly as possible. He gulped a few mouthfuls of soup, answered his comrade's question with a hurried shake of the head and rushed off. As he arrived back breathless at his control column it was just 1520 hours and the loudspeaker was announcing an order from the First Officer:

"From IO to all stations: Report to IO after meal."

Shortly afterwards the artillery telephone was heard again:

"Intensified look-out!"

Gödde turned his apparatus into the arc ahead. "The contact cruiser," he murmured to himself as another distance report reached the control position from the after Radar. "If only we could shake her off! Let's hope it's clear ahead, anyhow."

He thought no more about the British Force reported in the morning. His job was to keep watch in the direction ahead and to port, and this he did conscientiously.

The sea was still rising, and the battleship was pitching more and more alarmingly. In the port IV 5·9 gun turret Ordinary Seaman First Class Sträter noticed the first cases of seasickness. Outside it was pitch dark, and the driving snow had, after a short interval, set in again with renewed fury.

The British dispatch concerning the second engagement of Force 1 with the *Scharnhorst* contains, among other things, the following details:

At 1024 hours the 10th Cruiser Squadron closed the convoy and met up with the 36th Destroyer Division. Then the cruisers—because of the danger of U-boats—zigzagged 10 miles ahead of the convoy, with the 36th Destroyer Division disposed ahead of the cruiser force as a screen.

Towards noon it became clear to Admiral Fraser in the *Duke of York* that owing to the fuel situation in the destroyers he would be obliged either to turn back or go on to Kola Inlet for refuelling. If the *Scharnhorst* had already been on her way back to base at this time, there would have been no chance of catching her.

At 1155 hours Admiral Fraser ordered the convoy to alter course to 125°, that is, more to the south, his idea being to keep the cruisers between the convoy and the *Scharnhorst*. At 1137 hours the *Norfolk* made contact with the German battleship by Radar at 27,000 yards, but lost it a few minutes later. Then at 1205 the *Belfast* picked up the *Scharnhorst*, this time at 30,500 yards. Vice-Admiral Burnett now concentrated the 36th Destroyer Division on his starboard bow and altered course to 100°. At 1221 hours the *Sheffield* reported "Enemy in sight" and Force 1 was ordered to open fire at a range of 11,000 yards.

At the same time the 36th Destroyer Division was ordered to attack with torpedoes. The destroyers, however, owing to the extraordinarily bad weather conditions which greatly reduced their speed, and to the fact that the *Scharnhorst* was all the time retreating, did not come within torpedo range at this stage of the battle. The *Musketeer* opened fire at a range of 7,000 yards at 1222 hours and continued firing for 14 minutes.

During this second action, at 1233 hours, the *Norfolk* received a serious hit through the barbette of her after turret "X", which put it out of action, and the turret's magazine had to be flooded as a precaution. A second shell hit the *Norfolk* amidships. All the cruiser's Radar apparatus became unserviceable except for one set of the Type 284. One officer and six ratings were killed and five ratings were seriously wounded. At the same time an 11-inch salvo straddled the *Sheffield* and pieces of shell—some the size of footballs—according to the British report—crashed inboard; smaller fragments also penetrated the ship at various places.

With the *Scharnhorst* retreating at 28 knots the range, which during the action had narrowed to 4½–8 miles, opened more and more. Vice-Admiral Burnett decided to check fire and shadow with the whole of Force 1 until the *Scharnhorst* could be engaged by Admiral Fraser with Force 2. The 10th Cruiser Squadron therefore increased speed to 28 knots so that from 1250 hours onwards the enemy range remained steady at 13,400 yards. The 36th Destroyer Division too continued the chase. Later the range between the *Scharnhorst* and the pursuing cruisers opened to 20,000 yards and then remained steady.

During the following three hours of pursuit the cruisers stayed together in close company and kept contact with the *Scharnhorst* by Radar at 7½ miles, just outside visibility range. The 36th Destroyer Division which, as already mentioned, had dropped somewhat astern, closed the range slightly, but owing to the heavy sea could not get within firing range.

The *Norfolk*, in spite of the heavy damage she had

sustained, kept up with Force 1. At 1603 hours she was obliged to reduce speed to fight a fire in a wing compartment, but at 1700 hours she rejoined Force 1 again. The *Sheffield* dropped back at 1610 hours and reported that her port inner shaft was out of action and that she would have to reduce speed to 10 knots for half an hour. Within eleven minutes, however, she was catching up again; but her slowing down prevented her from rejoining Force 1 until 2100 hours. For the rest of the operation she remained some ten miles astern and followed the movements of the battle.

# XIII

## ADMIRAL SIR BRUCE FRASER
## CLOSES THE NET

ADMIRAL Sir Bruce Fraser, sailing in the *Duke of York* and acting on enemy reports received from Vice-Admiral Burnett, had on this December 26th been proceeding eastward with Force 2. His sole aim was to approach the *Scharnhorst*, cut off her retreat to Norway and sink her, thus disposing of the most serious threat to the Arctic convoys.

A quarter of an hour after the *Scharnhorst* had been engaged by the cruisers of the 10th Squadron, one of the young officers from the Radar plot of the *Duke of York* reported in the chart-house of the Admiral's bridge:

"Enemy reconnaissance aircraft, Sir."

The Admiral, who with his Chief-of-Staff had been checking Vice-Admiral Burnett's reports on the first action just concluded, looked up quickly:

"German reconnaissance aircraft? Where?"

"Eight and a half miles on the starboard quarter, Sir. We picked them up by Radar as well as by D/F. Three aircraft. One of the planes must have Radar; it's started sending radio location signals and is transmitting reports."

Sir Bruce exchanged glances with his Chief-of-Staff and placed the report sheet on the chart before him:

"Nothing else? No further signals?"

The Sub-Lieutenant shook his head:

"No, Sir. We're keeping contact with the aircraft."

I

"Good. Thank you."

The Radar officer left the room while the Chief-of-Staff noted down the position of the reconnaissance aircraft. Sir Bruce dropped into one of the heavy leather chairs and took up the report again:

"Our Radar arrangements are working well. It's vital that the officers in the Radar plot should keep in the closest possible touch with me. Don't you agree?"

The Chief-of-Staff nodded:

"I certainly do, Sir."

The Admiral was thoughtful for a moment, then taking up a ruler and striking the chart-table in emphasis as he spoke, said:

"In view of the importance of our Radar reports I shall for the rest of the operation divide my time between the Admiral's bridge and the plot. If an action develops and the situation becomes critical my place is obviously on the bridge; then you must remain in the plot and see to it that I get every scrap of information as soon as it becomes available. Is that clear?"

"Aye, aye, Sir. Let's hope we get the *Scharnhorst* today," the Chief-of-Staff added doubtfully.

"I am absolutely convinced of it," declared the Admiral, taking his pipe from his pocket.

Hours passed. The second engagement of the *Scharnhorst* by Force 1 had by now taken place. The British Commander-in-Chief was still uncertain whether the *Scharnhorst* too was accompanied by destroyers as the reports from the cruiser squadron after the first engagement had indicated. Then came the report from Vice-Admiral Burnett that the *Scharnhorst* was alone. There were no German destroyers with the battleship.

For about four hours the *Duke of York's* Radar observed the German reconnaissance aircraft shadowing the Force and sending out signals. Then it was seen no more; either it had lost contact or had returned to base.

At 1400 hours Sir Bruce sought out his Chief-of-Staff in the plotting-room. "I'm beginning to wonder," he said, "if our respective positions have been incorrectly reported. They seem too good to be true."

The Chief-of-Staff pointed with conviction to the large-scale chart on which all data were precisely recorded as they came in:

"Impossible, Sir. The D/F bearings here fully confirm the positions. Our approach is being made on a steady bearing."

Sir Bruce was relieved. "If the *Scharnhorst* maintains roughly her present course, she will run directly across our bows. I shall attack with the *Jamaica* on the same course, open fire at 13,000 yards and at the same time give the escort destroyers the order for torpedo attack. Burnett is keeping excellent contact."

The Chief-of-Staff traced with his pencil the course of the 10th Cruiser Squadron, Vice-Admiral Burnett's Force 1.

"Up to now, Sir, there's no indication that the reports of the German reconnaissance aircraft have influenced the movements of the *Scharnhorst* in the slightest. If she continues as she's going now," he cast a quick glance at his watch, "we shall be in action with her at about 1715 hours."

About two hours later, at 1617 hours, the Admiral was seated on a metal stool by the rapidly rotating disc which permitted a clear view through the large window of the bridge in spite of the driving snow, when suddenly one of the officers from the plotting-room appeared before him like a spirit conjured from the darkness.

"We've got her, Sir! The first report has just come in: 45,000 yards, bearing 020°. The Chief-of-Staff wishes to report that the bearing agrees with the plotted course. The *Scharnhorst* has turned on to a rather more southerly course. Force 1 has made the same report."

The Admiral jumped to his feet:

"Splendid; well done, Radar. Flag-Lieutenant: Pass on this Radar report with our own position to all ships!"

"Yes, Sir," came the voice of the Flag-Lieutenant out of the darkness.

Exactly twenty minutes later, at 1637 hours, the escorting destroyers received the order to take up the most advantageous positions for torpedo attack in sub-divisions. (Sub-divisions stationed on either bow of the *Duke of York* had previously been formed.) At the same time it was reported that the Radar had also picked up the *Belfast* which was coming up behind the *Scharnhorst* in pursuit.

Five minutes earlier, the *Duke of York's* fire-control Radar had found the *Scharnhorst* at 29,700 yards.

Sir Bruce gave a further order to the Flag-Lieutenant and requested the Captain of the flagship to come to the voice-pipe connecting the Admiral's bridge with the ship's bridge below. When Captain Russell reported, the Admiral himself was already standing at the voice-pipe:

"In two minutes Force 2 will turn to 80°, Russell. You can then bring all heavy guns to bear at once."

At 1647 hours the *Belfast* opened fire with starshell. One minute later, at 1648 hours, the *Duke of York* joined in also with starshell, and at 1650 hours the first heavy salvo thundered from the ten 14-inch barrels of the British flagship. The *Jamaica* followed with her twelve 6-inch guns, while the *Norfolk* and the *Belfast* opened fire somewhat later. The initial range was 12,000 yards.

# XIV

## THE *SCHARNHORST* UNDER FIRE

STATIONED at his control column, P.O. Gödde, who was searching slowly and systematically from dead ahead to the port beam, became suddenly aware that the Radar reports were taking a new shape. He took his eyes from the lenses, all attention now on the headphones. What was that? The after Radar, which had been putting through in routine fashion reports on the British ship shadowing astern, had suddenly discovered another target to starboard. And now, at the Captain's request, it was reporting the range and bearing of the new target. The P.O. suddenly recalled what the Captain had announced to all stations at 1130 hours: that an enemy Force was 150 miles away. Gödde pondered on this. Three hours previously the *Scharnhorst* had turned on to her present south-easterly course; before that she had been in the second action with the cruiser squadron. What would be the speed of this new Force? Twenty-eight to 30 knots, Gödde thought. That would mean 90 miles in the last three hours at the most. But this Force would obviously have been receiving continuous reports on the speed, course and position of the *Scharnhorst*—from the shadowing cruiser; hence, Gödde reasoned, if the enemy are out to intercept us on our return journey, they will have been able to take a short cut. This battle group must now be just about ready to strike.

Suddenly the piercing sound of the alarm bells shrieked through the ship.

It was 1600 hours.

In the port IV 5·9 twin turret Sträter heard the Signals-Transmitter read an announcement from the Captain:

"From the Captain to all stations! We are not yet out of the wood! Intensify the look-out! As you all know we have had a shadowing ship on our trail since noon and have not been able to shake her off. The Radar has just reported targets to starboard. Be prepared; keep on the alert. It may be any moment now."

The men in the turret listened keenly. Could it be an enemy force? Voices were raised:

"Where are they coming from? What sort of ships are they?"

A petty officer explained:

"It will be the Force reported this morning, boys, the one the aircraft spotted. It's already been announced."

"Things are getting hot," one of the men said. There was a short silence, then the Signals-Transmitter repeated an announcement from the Gunnery Commander:

"Shadows ahead!"

And immediately after that:

"To all stations: we are turning on to an easterly course!"

Heeling over heavily, the *Scharnhorst* slewed round and increased speed at the same time. The unbearable pitching changed into rolling, then into a soft rhythmical swaying now that the battleship was almost running before the sea again.

The Signals-Transmitter passed on a further announcement from the Gunnery Commander:

"Enemy opening fire to starboard. A.A. crews below deck. Skeleton crew only to remain on deck."

Then it came. Blow upon blow. In a matter of seconds ship and crew were swept along in the confused headlong rush of events. Gödde observed gigantic splashes

100 to 150 yards on his port side from what must have been shells of the heaviest calibre. Then, while the battleship was still turning round, her own heavy turrets opened fire. Gödde heard the Second Gunnery Officer, Kapitänleutnant Wieting, order single guns of the starboard secondary armament to fire starshell in between salvoes, evidently with the idea of enabling the visual range-finders to pick up the enemy. The enemy's own starshell firing seemed to slacken during the few starshell salvoes of the German 5·9-inch guns. The P.O. now heard an interchange between the Gunnery Commander and the Second Gunnery Officer on the artillery telephone. The Gunnery Commander thought it inadvisable to take guns from the batteries and thus weaken the defensive fire. The Second Gunnery Officer accordingly stopped the firing of starshell, and the guns which were ready for the next salvo were at once unloaded.

The enemy's shells which had been falling to port and starboard of the *Scharnhorst*, now began to fall wide and well behind the ship.

Anxiously Gödde searched for an enemy on the port side. Nothing could be seen but the glistening white columns of water which rose steeple-high as the 14-inch shells hit the sea. They rose from the water like pale phantoms trailing white shrouds, stood poised for a while and then fell in mighty cascades of water. The German heavy armament kept up continuous fire from all triple turrets.

At 1655 hours a 14-inch shell hit the starboard bows abreast of "A" turret and the blast threw P.O. Gödde to the deck. Overcome with shock and the greenish-black lyddite fumes he gasped for air and lay for several seconds on the wooden grating of his small platform, incapable of moving. Just at this moment the Captain appeared. The lenses of the optical apparatus had become temporarily unusable—from the effects of the hit and the fumes—and had to be cleaned from the outside by ratings sent up from below. Captain Hintze saw the prostrate man and helped him to his feet:

"Are you wounded, Gödde?"

The P.O. pulled himself together:

"No, Herr Kapitän, only stunned."

The Captain pointed to the apparatus:

"Stay at your post. We can't afford to be taken by surprise from this side."

"A" turret was now jammed in its bearings with its barrels elevated and could no longer be trained. Shortly after the first hit, a second was scored amidships.

Later, when Gödde's artillery-telephone had been put out of action, and he had switched over to the ship-control telephone system, he heard a report from one of the stations to the Gunnery Commander:

"A" turret is no longer reporting. Fire and smoke around the turret prevent entry."

This meant that "A" turret was completely out of action and that the *Scharnhorst's* defences were deprived of three 11-inch guns. Her remaining heavy guns, six 11-inch barrels, meanwhile stepped up their fire to a quick succession of salvoes and the range opened to 17,000–20,000 yards. It was observed that the enemy was frequently straddled by salvoes and that many near misses fell close to the British ship. This gunnery duel lasted some twenty minutes and was conducted by both sides with the utmost ferocity. Throughout this period a continuous stream of starshell were exploding over the *Scharnhorst*. The flares hung over the ship for minutes on end like so many huge floodlights exposing everything with stark, pitiless clarity, the cruel brilliance sharpened by the fiery flashes of the German's own salvoes. The whole battleship from bridges to foretop, masts and funnels was bathed in a ghastly pink to blood-red light. Smoke and cordite fumes clung to the ship, driven now by an almost following wind, and at times completely obscured visibility in the direction of the enemy. Through the thunder of the German salvoes the British shells could be heard screaming over and thudding into the sea, while those that met their target caused the ship, already rocked by the recoil of her own guns, to tremble from stem to stern.

P.O. Gödde concluded from the gunnery orders that the range was opening while German and British fire slackened appreciably. The *Scharnhorst* was steady on her easterly course and seemed to increase speed still more. The intervals between salvoes lengthened and visibility gradually improved.

As the action was being fought to starboard the crews in the port IV 5·9-inch twin turret could open the turret trap-hatch occasionally and observe the continuous explosion of starshell over the ship stabbing the darkness with their glare. At 1650 hours the turret Signals-Transmitter repeated an announcement from the Captain:

"From the Captain to all stations. The heavy enemy units are turning away, they can't match our speed." Then after a short pause: "The *Scharnhorst* has again proved herself."

For a while the men in the turret could hear the *Scharnhorst's* guns still firing. Then they too checked fire.

"Whew!" a voice commented from the depths of the turret, "this time we only just made it."

But they had had only a foretaste of what was to come. That they did not realize this, was perhaps merciful.

At the beginning of this engagement the British Forces were disposed in the following manner:

The *Duke of York* and the *Jamaica* were steering to the southward of the *Scharnhorst*. Behind the German battleship, which had at once turned round to an easterly course, followed the remaining units of Force 2: the destroyers *Savage* and *Saumarez* on her port quarter, and *Scorpion* and *Stord* on her starboard quarter. The *Belfast* and *Norfolk* attacked from the north. The *Sheffield*, which was still astern of Force 1, dropped slowly back owing to her reduced speed and could take no part in the action. The 36th Destroyer Division standing to the north-westward of the *Scharnhorst*, also changed course at 1700 hours to follow the *Scharnhorst* on her eastward flight and crept forward to take up the most favourable position for delivering its torpedo attacks from the north. *Musketeer* hoped to synchronize these attacks with those to be launched by the destroyer screen of Force 2 closing in on the opposite side, but a technical failure in the *Musketeer's* W/T equipment prevented her from establishing wireless communication with *Savage* (which was leading the destroyer screen of Force 2).

During this initial action of Force 2, according to Admiral Sir Bruce Fraser's dispatch, no hits were scored on the British units.

# XV

## THE DESTROYER SUB-DIVISIONS
## OF FORCE 2 ATTACK

THE stages of the battle which now follow, leading up to the sinking of the *Scharnhorst*, are extremely difficult to piece together in all their detail as the few German eye-witness accounts available do not entirely agree. This is understandable, for in a comparatively short space of time the *Scharnhorst* was attacked again and again from all sides, rocked and pounded by heavy gunfire and torpedoes while keeping up her own uninterrupted fire to the very end.

The survivors—all petty officers or ratings—were throughout the turmoil chained to their respective posts and had practically no opportunity of gaining an overall impression of what was happening. The author has therefore accepted Admiral Sir Bruce Fraser's sober and objective dispatch as the best guide to the chronological sequence of events.

The lull following the Captain's last announcement, during which the *Scharnhorst's* heavy artillery temporarily checked fire, lasted only five to ten minutes. Then once more the ship was exposed to the dazzling light of starshell and the heavy shock of an underwater explosion, amidships on the starboard side, shuddered through her hull. Soon after this her speed slackened.

In the port IV 5·9-inch turret the Signals-Transmitter passed on the report:

"Torpedo hit in boiler-room 1. Speed 8 knots."

Inside the turret the men heard that the starboard secondary armament was now firing. At the same time, scarcely audible in the noise of battle, the A.A. guns on the upper deck, manned by the skeleton crews, started to fire. A report came up from the shell magazine:

"Smoke developing!"

Staff Chief-Gunner Wibbelhoff turned to his crew:

"Gas masks on!"

Scarcely had the men slipped on their masks than the Signals-Transmitter was heard again:

"From starboard I—5·9-inch turret: Shell hit in magazine. Gun out of action. Magazine personnel dead."

Calmly, deliberately, as learned in long battle training, the seaman passed the message on. The men in the turret were not surprised when immediately after this came the order for the starboard I gun:

"Gun platform of starboard I—5·9-inch, fall in at the forward personnel assembly centre."

Crews of disabled guns were redistributed to other guns, formed into fire-fighting units or drafted as working parties to armoured positions, a routine which had been practised often enough in battle exercises.

Now the German heavy armament began firing again. The men could clearly distinguish the after "C" turret, firing together with the after guns of the secondary armament. Half a minute later the order to fire came for the starboard IV 5·9-inch twin turret. The men in the turret sighed with relief when the Signals-Transmitter with raised voice and beaming face shouted through the noise and smoke:

"To all stations: we're doing 22 knots again."

Unaware that they had just heard the last bit of good news that their Signals-Transmitter would be called upon to pass on, they silently blessed their shipmates at work down below on the boilers and turbines.

P.O. Gödde, standing at his control column, heard the reports of the enemy's movements as they flowed in at the control position. New British units were appearing constantly. He observed that this attack was being delivered by destroyers. First they hove in sight as mere shadows, then their shapes and outlines became visible. Those coming up in the *Scharnhorst's* wake were clearly visible. Evidently there were others to starboard. This he could infer from the defensive fire of the secondary armament and the A.A. guns which were now barking ferociously though somewhat irregularly. And all the time, through this phase of the battle the *Scharnhorst* was again mercilessly illuminated by star-shell which, fired from every side, thrust her, stark and bare, out of the darkness and whirling snow. When the pursuing destroyers had come to within about two cables of the *Scharnhorst*, Gödde noted with satisfaction that "C" turret was now joining the after 5·9-inch turrets and the after 4·1-inch A.A. guns in defensive fire. Then he too heard the glad news that the *Scharnhorst* had again increased her speed to 22 knots.

Half an hour after the beginning of the first gun duel it still seemed to the British Commander-in-Chief that it was possible for the *Scharnhorst* to escape. Everything now depended upon the four "S" class destroyers, i.e. the two sub-divisions forming the screen of Force 2. At 1731 hours they received the order to attack with torpedoes and on the Radar screen Sir Bruce himself observed how the two sub-divisions crept gradually into torpedo range and manœuvred into the firing position. As the Admiral could not be certain whether the destroyers would indeed be able to close in, he had already decided to turn towards the Norwegian coast, hoping that the *Scharnhorst* would be led into altering course accordingly and so give his destroyers a good opportunity to attack with torpedo. The German battleship's loss of speed, however, made this stratagem superfluous.

By 1840 hours the first sub-division (*Savage* and *Saumarez*) were astern of the *Scharnhorst*; at the same time the second sub-division (*Scorpion* and *Stord*) closed in from the south-east to about 10,000 yards, and were on the *Scharnhorst's* starboard beam ready to fire their torpedoes. The *Scharnhorst* opened heavy fire against the *Savage* and *Saumarez* with her secondary armament and A.A. guns which the two destroyers returned. At the same time they fired starshell. The second sub-division *Scorpion* and *Stord* turned for the torpedo attack, *Scorpion* firing eight torpedoes at 2,100 yards and *Stord* another eight at 1,800 yards. *Scorpion* observed one hit. The *Scharnhorst*, turning to south-ward ostensibly to get out of the line of fire, put herself just where the first sub-division wanted her. Thus, while the second sub-division on its retreat came under heavy secondary armament and A.A. fire from the *Scharnhorst*, the first sub-division hastily trained its torpedo tubes from port to starboard and turned in to attack. *Savage* fired her eight torpedoes at a range of 3,500 yards. *Saumarez*, which owing to casualties and damage had only one set of tubes clear for action, and lying as she was under heavy fire, could launch only four torpedoes at 1,800 yards.

*Savage* remained miraculously intact, but *Saumarez* was damaged above the waterline and sustained casu-alties. Shells hit her director and penetrated below her range-finder director without however exploding. Splinters from other shells caused further damage which reduced her speed to ten knots on one engine only. One officer and ten ratings were killed and eleven ratings wounded. *Savage* claimed to have observed three hits on the *Scharnhorst*, *Saumarez* one.

The attack of the two sub-divisions was carried out without support from the *Duke of York* or the *Jamaica*. The *Duke of York* observed three heavy underwater explosions on the *Scharnhorst*, the *Belfast* six—an indication of how uncertain and unreliable observations made during a night action are, though they may be made and reported in good faith.

After delivering their attacks the destroyers withdrew to the northward.

# XVI

## THE *DUKE OF YORK* ATTACKS FOR THE SECOND TIME; FORCE 2 AND FORCE 1 CLOSE IN FOR THE FINAL BATTLE

WHILE the *Scharnhorst's* heavy guns were still firing at the retreating destroyers, P.O. Gödde heard the after Radar reporting new targets; the Captain asked for their respective bearings and ranges, and these were given.

Shortly afterwards the 11-inch guns opened fire on these as yet shadowy opponents, one of which was soon identified as a battleship; heavy shells fell into the sea around the *Scharnhorst*. The Second Gunnery Officer, Kapitänleutnant Wieting, ordered the secondary armament to open fire on the battleship and on a second opponent which, judging by its shell calibre, was obviously a cruiser.

Hit upon hit crashed on to the *Scharnhorst*. Heavy explosions followed one upon the other, and as each bout of violent rocking subsided it was replaced by a slow vibration as if the very hull were trembling. Steel crashed upon steel; fire broke out and the smoke which billowed from the quickly spreading flames mingled with the acrid cordite fumes of the German salvoes and the strangely stinging odour from the British explosives. The two remaining triple turrets kept up their relentless fire in company with the 5·9-inch battery and the 4·1-inch A.A. guns. Between the German salvoes one could hear the dull rumbling noise of starshell exploding over the battleship, the detonations of torpedoes and the impact of shells. The rending steel groaned and hissing splinters hammered like hail on superstructures and decks. The enemy's wide shots came screaming over the *Scharnhorst* and fell with heavy thuds into the sea beyond, flooding decks and guns with the swell and marking their trail with a rain of deadly splinters.

This hurricane of fire, this ghastly concentration of assault from heavy guns and torpedoes, took place—according to the British dispatch—between 1901 and 1937 hours.

In the fearful din of battle in which the *Scharnhorst* was now enveloped, none but the well-trained ear, tried in exercise and action, could distinguish voices and interpret the reports and orders which the ship's telephone system was picking up from every side. P.O. Gödde possessed such a practised ear. He had his eyes pressed closely to the lenses of his control column, raising them only occasionally to look round him, when a particularly heavy explosion shook the ship. Through the noise came word from the Captain:

*"Scharnhorst immer voran!"*

It was the ship's motto. Gödde gritted his teeth and looked up. He realized that the long bows of the *Scharnhorst* had nosed straight into the path of a shell. The noise of the explosion mingled with the sight of wood, iron and steel torn asunder as by giant, flaming ploughshares. Then the blast flung the P.O. from his apparatus, lifted him bodily into the air and threw him violently on to the deck. Gödde lost consciousness and lay inert. When he wearily opened his eyes again he saw the Captain.

Captain Hintze had left the control position through the port door opposite Gödde's control column to take a quick look round. The lenses of the optical instruments in the control position had for the most part been destroyed by flying shrapnel; the rest had been made temporarily unserviceable by clinging snow, water and slime. Just as the Captain was squeezing through the narrow aperture of the slightly open armoured door, the 14-inch shell—the one which tore Gödde from the control column—hit the bows. Splinters grazed the Captain's face but he seemed hardly to notice them. He had only the sensation of something warm trickling down his forehead and on to his cheeks and he dabbed it with his handkerchief. Then he saw Gödde crumpled up on the wooden slats of the control column platform. He bent over him:

"Are you wounded, Gödde?"

The same question as he had asked the P.O. two hours previously. The Captain helped the prostrate man to his feet. Gödde rubbed his eyes and looked at his apparatus.

"No, Sir. It was only a few splinters. The gear's all right."

The Captain nodded:

"Good. See what's wrong with the starboard control column. It's not answering."

With this the Captain withdrew once more to the control position and Gödde hurried round to the other control column. In the harsh light of starshell one glance sufficed. The men on the platform were all dead. The apparatus was totally destroyed. All that remained was an unrecognizable mass of twisted steel, shattered instruments and torn, half-melted cables. As quickly as he could Gödde rushed back to his own control column, slipped on his telephone and reported:

"Starboard forward control column destroyed. Crew dead."

This hit must have occurred a few minutes after 1900 hours. About twenty minutes later, roughly at

1925 hours, Gödde felt the impact of a torpedo which brought the battleship practically to a standstill. Then a shell of medium calibre, fired no doubt by one of the cruisers now stationed to the north and south of the *Scharnhorst*, crashed into her bows. A fragment of this smashed the upper mobile portion of the control column at which Gödde was stationed and flung it from its bearings, while other splinters severed the cables of the head-phone. He himself remained unscathed. While Gödde was still occupied in investigating the damage a Quartermaster sent out by the Captain appeared:

"The Captain wants to know what's happened here? Why don't you answer?"

"The control column's gone. And the telephone too."

The Quartermaster disappeared into the control position again and then returned once more.

"Order from the Captain: Come into the control position. The old man says there's no point in staying outside any longer."

Casting a last look at the shambles around him, Gödde followed the Quartermaster and squeezed himself through the armoured door into the control position.

# XVII

## IN THE CONTROL POSITION AND PORT IV 5·9-INCH TWIN TURRET OF THE *SCHARNHORST*

A FLOOD of reports was streaming into the control position without a break. By the light of the gun flashes from "B" turret which, coming through the periscopes, illuminated the dimness of the control tower, P.O. Gödde recognized the tall figure of the First Officer. Fregattenkapitän Dominik had come up from the Commander's office to the control position to report to the Captain. Rear-Admiral Bey, massive and broad-shouldered, was leaning against the starboard wall. The narrow viewing-slits of the control tower were closed by armoured shutters as in any case nothing now could be seen through them. There were three periscopes in the control position, one of which was for the Quartermaster, fitted with the excellent, highly sensitive Bremen Atlas lenses as indeed were all the optical instruments on board. In the midst of the din, the engine-room telephone was heard:

"From Chief Engineer to Captain. Third engine out of action through defect in steam-supply. Hope to repair damage in twenty to thirty minutes."

In well under twenty minutes the report came through from the engine-room:

"From Chief Engineer to Captain: Ship can do twenty knots again."

Captain Hintze tapped the Signals-Transmitter on the shoulder:

"Transmit: To Chief Engineer from Captain Hintze: Well done, engine-room! The ship's officers and men thank you for your good work."

He made a quick sign to the Officer-of-the-Watch, the engine-room telegraphs rattled and the *Scharnhorst*, which for a while had been almost stationary, gathered way. Rear-Admiral Bey went over to the Captain and Gödde saw Admiral, Captain and First Officer exchange a few words. Finally the Commander-in-Chief gestured to starboard:

"Turn north, Hintze. Perhaps we can get out of this inferno that way."

It was about 1920 hours when Admiral Bey gave the command.

The *Scharnhorst* was turning from her westerly course to the northward when the Captain beckoned to the Torpedo Officer. Gödde knew from previous exchanges he had overheard that Captain Hintze, as torpedo specialist of long standing, had throughout the action been considering the use of torpedoes. Oberleutnant Bosse, the *Scharnhorst's* Torpedo Officer, briefly raised his hand to his cap:

"I have just heard, Herr Kapitän, that the training-gear and tie-rods of the port set have been destroyed by direct hits. The starboard set has also been damaged by a hit amidships. A messenger reported, as all communications aft have been severed. I will see if, with my torpedo P.O. artificer, I can get the tubes into working order. I will report at once when everything is clear."

"Good, Bosse," answered the Captain. "The firing of the torpedoes is to be left to my discretion. Wait for my orders. See to it that things are put right as quickly as possible."

"*Jawohl*, Herr Kapitän! I'll do my best!"

Oberleutnant Bosse left the control position and

clambered down the port companion-way to the upper deck.

The telephone buzzed again, this time from the Commander's office to which the First Officer had returned after the change of course:

"From First Officer to Captain: forward dressing-station destroyed. Ship's doctor, Chaplain and entire personnel killed."

The forward dressing-station lay close behind the Commander's office, deep below the control position.

Things had been quiet in the port IV 5·9-inch twin turret during the initial phase of the last action. Only the starboard secondary armament was still firing apart from the triple turrets "B" and "C" and the A.A. guns. Sträter and his comrades could hear the reports of the guns and feel the impact of the enemy onslaught and were desperately anxious to throw their weight into the battle. They listened breathlessly to the bulletins which the turret Signals-Transmitter relayed after every serious blow.

"Starboard II—5·9-inch reports: hit; gun can be trained to a limited extent only."

And a few minutes later:

"Starboard II—5·9-inch: out of action from another hit."

When the Captain's exhortation "*Scharnhorst immer voran*" reached them, they looked at each other and smiled. They knew that every section of the crew was doing its utmost to honour their ship's motto. But the smiles left their faces when within a few seconds the ship was struck with unprecedented force and began to tremble violently along her entire length. The emergency lamps fell from their mountings; the men set to and replaced them as further heavy explosions occurred. They looked at their Signals-Transmitter questioningly. He shook his head:

"Nothing's come through so far."

"That was a torpedo hit," said Chief Petty Officer Moritz, the Chief Gunner. "It couldn't have been anything else."

They fell silent. At length the Signals-Transmitter had another bulletin:

"'B' turret to damage control party: Order to flood! Magazine chamber 'B' turret to be flooded."

The men listened aghast: was "B" turret also out of action now? "A" turret had remained jammed since the first encounter with the British battleship. Must "B" go too . . . ? But then they heard "B" turret firing again, distant and subdued, but clearly recognizable. Enveloped in smoke and fumes it was to keep firing to the very last. The men relaxed again.

It was not until he was in captivity that Sträter learned from Able Seaman Birkle, another survivor, what had actually happened. Birkle was a member of the gun crew of "B" turret. "A" turret had received a severe hit—the second of the day—in its magazine chamber. Violent explosions had followed, the smoke of which had completely enveloped "B" and red-hot splinters had penetrated the bulkheads protecting the magazines. The Chief Gunner took the immediate and reasonable precaution of having the magazines flooded. It had, however, proved possible to pump them out again a quarter of an hour later.

In the port IV 5·9-inch twin turret they were still discussing the possible consequences of this when a further heavy shock was felt.

"Hit in the aircraft hangar," called the Signals-Transmitter. "Severe fire. A.A. crews to fight fire in the hangar."

They heard the A.A. crews hurrying along. They even felt the heat of the fire in their own turret which was situated one deck lower abreast the rear portion of the hangar. Then they heard the orders of the officers and petty officers in charge of fire-fighting. Meanwhile the Captain's announcement had reached them:

"Ship making twenty knots again."

But the port battery had still received no order to fire. The crew followed with strained attention every incident which could give them a clue as to how the battle was going. They noticed how the *Scharnhorst* gradually gathered speed again; as they felt her heel over, they guessed she was changing course, they correctly interpreted the transition from the pitching movement into a quiet regular roll as the return on to a northerly course. And at last came the long awaited order to fire which Kapitänleutnant Wieting, the Second Gunnery Officer, transmitted from the forward control position:

"Target: enemy gun flashes somewhat before the beam."

Precise bearings, range and lateral deflection followed. In no time Chief Gunner Moritz brought the pointers into line and trained the turret.

"Six seconds interval between salvoes. Fire ... !"

Only Staff Chief Gunner Wibbelhoff and the Chief Gunner could, with the aid of periscopes, see the enemy. All the rest were, so to speak, blind. They manned their two guns and went all out to keep up the pace of firing. Sweat streamed from their blistered brows into their eyes; their bodies were soaked.

"The 4·1-inch are shooting with starshell," the Signals-Transmitter roared through the turmoil. And shortly after that:

"Heavy guns report: ammunition exhausted! 'B' turret has three shots left, 'C' turret none."

Doggedly they worked on, swung the full loading-trays behind the breeches, loaded, fired, tore the breeches open, caught the smoking brass cartridges as they clattered from the fuming barrels and threw them through the apertures to the deck below, fired, loaded, fired. Ceaselessly the munition hoists rattled up and down, the fire-gong shrieked and the guns thundered.

"Order to 'C' turret," the voice of the Signals-Transmitter roared through the din. "Carry ammunition astern from magazines 'A' turret."

And then:

"From Captain to secondary armament: It's up to you now! The heavy guns are out of action!"

While the 5·9-inch guns, still intact, went on firing, the turret Signals-Transmitter called:

"From Third Gunnery Officer to Gunnery Commander: Control of 'C' turret by Third Gunnery Officer from after control position by means of emergency line."

They knew now that Kapitänleutnant Fügner, the Third Gunnery Officer, was going to bring the after triple turret back into action.

A few minutes after the after "C" turret had ceased firing owing to lack of ammunition the thunder of its 11-inch barrels was again roaring above the barking of the secondary armament. They'd done it again! They had carried ammunition aft, to where the Third Gunnery Officer, Kapitänleutnant Fügner, now continued to direct firing from the after control position until the battleship went down.

The Signals-Transmitter in the port IV turret raised his hand:

"From the Captain to all stations: Wireless signal to Supreme Command. The *Scharnhorst* will go on fighting to the last shell. Long live the Führer! Long live Germany!"

They knew then that the end was near.

# XVIII

## JAMAICA, BELFAST AND THE BRITISH DESTROYERS SINK THE SCHARNHORST WITH TORPEDOES

IT was the British torpedoes which finally brought about the end of the German battleship.

One, two torpedo detonations thundered above the indescribable pandemonium of the battle and the *Scharnhorst* slowly took a list to starboard. Whatever there was that could still fire—"C" turret and the remaining 5·9-inch guns—went on firing. And again two, three torpedo detonations crashed forth. They hit on the starboard side and the list increased. Simultaneously came the order:

"From the Captain to all stations. Destroy all secret papers and installations. To damage control party: prepare for scuttling! All men detailed for scuttling to their stations!"

More violent explosions. Torpedoes again. The port 20-mm. A.A. gun was still firing from the fore-top, the only one which had remained in action after the fore-top had been hit during the morning. It fired down from the main A.A. gun tower and with it the port IV 5·9-inch twin turret. Then, because of the heavy list, the hoist in the twin turret jammed in its shaft. At the same time the order was passed down from the bridge:

"Abandon ship."

Staff Chief Gunner Wibbelhoff rose from his seat:

"Leave the turret!" he ordered.

The men hesitated. During the whole operation the turret had suffered neither damage nor casualties.

"Leave the turret, boys," Wibbelhoff repeated, raising his voice. "I'm staying where I belong."

Chief Petty Officer Moritz went at once to Wibbelhoff's side:

"I'm staying too."

Not another word was spoken. Slowly the men turned away and prepared to leave, returning the Battery Commander's last salute.

They clambered out slowly one after the other, still a little uncertain, turning round for a last glance. Sträter, one of the last to leave, saw Wibbelhoff put his hand in his pocket and quietly produce a packet of cigarettes. He saw him light up and in the calm deliberate manner so familiar to his men, swing back into his seat. Moritz likewise lowered himself on to his laying-seat. Sträter felt a lump in his throat as he gazed on the scene for the last time, a scene which was to be indelibly printed on his mind and swim before his eyes whenever he thought of his ship.

Both men were still at their stations when the *Scharnhorst* capsized and sank.

Shortly before the first torpedoes of this last phase of the battle hit the *Scharnhorst*, Gödde, now in the control position, heard that enemy destroyers were closing from astern.

The Captain, who received the report, looked at the Commander-in-Chief:

"They want to finish us off like the *Bismarck*, Herr Admiral. Torpedoes into rudder and screws!"

He stepped to the side of the Signals-Transmitter at the emergency line which the Torpedo Officer, now standing by at the torpedo tubes, had had hurriedly laid. Then Captain Hintze gave the order to fire torpedoes. By a supreme effort, the Torpedo Officer, Oberleutnant Bosse, and those of his men who were left, had carried out emergency repairs on the damaged tubes; now with the help of a few ratings, he succeeded in training them and firing torpedoes first to port, then to starboard at the targets indicated by the Captain. After the appropriate interval the stern look-out reported to the control position that he had observed a brilliant blaze astern.

According to British sources this was yet another of the mistaken claims made in good faith by both sides during the night battle.

The *Scharnhorst* was hit by the first enemy torpedo salvo at about 1927 hours, and six minutes later, at 1933 hours, by the second. Four minutes after that, at about 1937 hours, the last torpedoes detonated with a thunderous roar against the ship's starboard side.

The fate of the *Scharnhorst* was sealed.

## XIX

## "TO ALL STATIONS. FROM THE
## CAPTAIN: ABANDON SHIP!"

GÖDDE, deeply moved, heard reports coming in from all parts of the dying ship; in accordance with the Captain's orders to prepare for scuttling, the damage control parties had fitted the explosive charges and one by one the various installations were being destroyed or rendered useless.

The *Scharnhorst* was listing more and more to starboard as Captain Hintze beckoned the Navigating Officer to him.

"Pass to the Action Information Centre," he ordered, "a last report of our position in clear text. Quickly Lanz. Time is running out!"

Then he gripped the Chief Signals-Transmitter by the arm:

'To all stations. From the Captain: Abandon ship. Every man to the upper deck. Life-jackets on. Prepare to jump overboard!"

Summoned by the Captain, the First Officer, Fregattenkapitän Dominik, had come up from the Commander's office through the armoured shaft. Rear-Admiral Bey, Captain and First Officer now discussed the measures still to be taken. Then Gödde saw the slim figure of the First Officer leaving the control position to go across the bay of the bridge and down the port companion-way to the upper deck. The list was becoming increasingly marked and Captain Hintze urged the twenty-five men in the control position to leave.

"Off with you, men. Put on your jackets. Just think of yourselves now. And don't forget to inflate them."

Most of them refused to leave without the Captain. A young rating shook his head and said simply:

"We're staying with you."

Another young rating said he had no life-jacket and that he too was staying in the position. The Captain unfastened his own life-jacket and took it off.

"Here you are," he said. "You have mine. I'm a good swimmer. But now off with you. I'll come afterwards, never fear."

The combined efforts of Commander-in-Chief and Captain succeeded at length in getting the men out of the position. Every one of them received a parting hand-shake from Rear-Admiral Bey and Captain Hintze, who then moved over to the bay of the bridge. From this vantage point the Captain looked silently down on to the upper deck which was swarming with men. They continued to flood from companion-ways and hatches to stand then in silent groups, waiting. Not a shout, not a sound was heard but the roar of the sea, the howling of the south-westerly gale and at intervals the dull explosion of single starshell as they still came over from the British ships.

So, with exemplary discipline the remnants of the crew assembled on deck among the dead who lay everywhere about them. There was nowhere the slightest sign of panic. They awaited further orders. Even the young cadets who with no previous battle experience had done their duty magnificently, raised their eyes to the bridge. Captain Hintze was holding a megaphone and now gave his instructions for leaving the ship.

"Don't go overboard to starboard, my friends. Go over from the port side, and slide from the rail into the water."

P.O. Gödde now saw the Gunnery Commander, Korvettenkapitän Bredenbreuker, and the Second Gunnery Officer, Kapitänleutnant Wieting, come out from the fire-control position and go on to the bay of the bridge. They walked over to the Captain, exchanged a few words with him, then left the bridge and went down over the port companion-way to the upper deck. The Captain lifted his megaphone again:

"Don't forget to inflate your life-jackets. And now, one after the other, over the rail."

The First Officer, towering a head above the others, stood below to pass on the Captain's orders and organize the going-overboard, helping each man personally. As Gödde prepared to leave the bridge, the *Scharnhorst* was rolling heavily in the rough sea and was enveloped in dense smoke and fumes, but she was still moving slowly. Her starboard side lay in the water practically to the folded wing of the bridge, while the highest waves washed the main mast. Snow squalls, mingled with hail, had again set in and starshell still hovered over the sinking ship.

Admiral Fraser's dispatch shows how the last phase of the action was planned on the basis of a concentration of all available British forces. The decisive factors in the destruction of the *Scharnhorst* were the superiority of British Radar technique, the heavier guns of the *Duke of York* (14-inch against 11-inch) and the determined attacks of all British destroyer sub-divisions.

The British Commander-in-Chief succeeded in concentrating all his forces against the *Scharnhorst* in the period from 1901 hours—when the *Duke of York* opened fire—to 1937 hours—when the *Jamaica* fired her last torpedo salvo. The firing of the guns and torpedoes which finally sank the *Scharnhorst* was timed as follows:

1901 hrs *Duke of York* and *Jamaica* opened fire.

Range: 10,400 yards.

*Norfolk* opened fire but checked after two salvoes owing to difficulty in seeing the *Scharnhorst*. Between 1901 and 1928 hours it was observed that the *Scharnhorst's* speed had fallen from 20 to 5 knots.

1915 hrs *Belfast* opened fire.

Range: 17,000 yards.

1925 hrs *Jamaica* fired three torpedoes to *Scharnhorst's* port side, one of which misfired.

Range: 3,500 yards.

No hit was observed, probably due to to the fact that the *Scharnhorst* appeared to the British to be stationary at this time.

1927 hrs *Belfast* fired three torpedoes to the *Scharnhorst's* starboard side.

Range: Not precisely indicated, but about the same as *Jamaica*, i.e. 3,500 yards.

One hit was reported which the British dispatch regards as improbable.

*Jamaica* and *Belfast* hauled round to fire their remaining torpedo tubes, *Jamaica* meanwhile engaging the *Scharnhorst* with gun fire.

1928 hrs *Duke of York* checked fire.

1931 hrs 72nd Sub-division of the 36th Destroyer Division (*Opportune* and *Virago*) attacked.

*Opportune* fired four torpedoes on *Scharnhorst's* starboard side.

Range: 2,100 yards.

One unobserved hit reported.

1933 hrs 71st Sub-division of the 36th Destroyer Division (*Musketeer* and *Matchless*, attacked from the northeast on *Scharnhorst's* port quarter; *Musketeer* fired four torpedoes.

Range: 1,000 yards.

Two, perhaps three, hits observed between funnel and main mast. *Matchless* followed, but could not deliver her attack as a heavy sea had hit her torpedo-mountings while the tubes were being trained from port to starboard. The training-gear was strained so badly that the attack could not be continued from this side. When *Matchless* hauled round and came in to attack again on the *Scharn-*

*horst's* port bow the battleship had already sunk and *Matchless* took part in picking up survivors.

1933 hrs *Opportune* of the 72nd Sub-division of the 36th Destroyer Division fired another salvo of four torpedoes.

Range: 2,500 yards.

One unobserved hit reported.

1934 hrs *Virago* of the 72nd Sub-division of the 36th Destroyer Division fired seven torpedoes.

Range: 2,800 yards.

Two hits observed.

While the destroyers were retiring, *Virago* opened up with gun fire.

1937 hrs *Jamaica* fired three torpedoes on *Scharnhorst's* port side.

Range: 3,750 yards.

Two hits reported as, after the appropriate interval, two underwater explosions were felt. They were not directly observed as the *Scharnhorst*, now almost at a standstill, was enveloped in clouds of smoke.

1948 hrs *Belfast* was about to attack with torpedoes, but refrained when, on firing starshell to illuminate the target, only drifting wreckage of the *Scharnhorst* was observed.

In the target area there were present at this time: one battleship, three cruisers and eight destroyers. The *Duke of York* withdrew to the northward to avoid the mêlée of ships. All that could be seen of the *Scharnhorst* was a dark glowing mass within an enormous cloud of smoke lit up by starshell and the searchlights of the surrounding ships. From the British side neither the glare of the starshell nor the beams of the searchlights could penetrate behind that smoke-cloud. Thus no ship actually saw the *Scharnhorst* sink. It seems certain however that she sank after a heavy underwater explosion which was heard and felt by various ships at 1945 hours.

*Jamaica*, *Matchless* and *Virago* were the last ships to sight the *Scharnhorst* (at 1938 hours). When the *Belfast* turned in for her second torpedo attack at 1948 hours the German battleship had finally sunk. She went down

L

in approximately 72° 16′ N., 28° 41′ E. The *Jamaica* joined the *Duke of York* on her northerly course while *Belfast*, *Norfolk* and most of the destroyers continued until 2040 hours to search for survivors. During this time *Scorpion* picked up thirty survivors and *Matchless*, six. *Scorpion* reported that the German Admiral and the *Scharnhorst's* Captain had been seen in the water seriously wounded. The Captain was dead before he could be reached. The Admiral grasped a life-line but died before he could be hauled on board.

Soon after 2100 hours *Sheffield* caught up with Force 1.

All forces in the area were ordered by Admiral Sir Bruce Fraser to proceed independently to Kola Inlet for refuelling where they arrived without incident on the following day, 27 December 1943.

The survivors picked up by the two destroyers were taken on board the *Duke of York* in Kola Inlet and were provisionally interrogated during the ship's return to Scapa Flow. Among them was not one commissioned officer. The senior in rank was Petty Officer Acting C.P.O. Gödde.

# XX

## THE RESCUE
## OF SURVIVORS BY THE BRITISH
## DESTROYERS
### *MATCHLESS* AND *SCORPION*

GÖDDE was still standing on the bay of the bridge. It was high time to leave, for the ship threatened to capsize at any moment. Next to him stood one of the petty officers of his own, the 3rd Division, Bo'sun's Mate Deierling. He looked on impatiently as Gödde fumbled with his life-jacket.

"Come here, man," he said. "Let me help you. You'll never get the thing on alone."

He helped Gödde to pull the straps under his arms and over his shoulders and tied the tapes for him.

The Captain showed his concern for the personnel of the control position and bridge to the very last. In the intervals between shouting instructions down to the upper deck through the megaphone, Captain Hintze examined the life-jacket of every single man.

The deck was already tilted at a steep angle, so Gödde and Deierling joined hands and moved carefully across the icy surface. As the port companion-way was crowded with men, they decided to use instead the starboard companion-way leading to the upper deck. The starboard bridge was already on a level with the water and heavy breakers lashed the main mast. Suddenly the two Petty Officers lost their footing and a receding wave swept them from the ship, separating them.

Gödde was drawn down by the suction around the hull. He felt an unbearable pressure in his ear drums, then he was tossed to the surface. He tried desperately to get clear of the whirling waters which eddied round the ship. Of Deierling there was no trace.

In front of him he saw an "otter"—one of the floats belonging to the battleship's mine-sweeping gear—with a man sitting astride it. Gödde swam towards the otter and his shipmate tried to pull him up, but the otter overturned and both men slipped back into the water. Gödde swam on and came across a large brass cartridge bobbing up and down in the water, one of the empty 11-inch cartridges. But when he tried to get a grip on its brassy surface, it moved away from him, filled with water and sank. Wooden gratings, washed away from the bridges, were drifting all about him in the heavy seas and Gödde succeeded in pushing one of them under his body. Laboriously he stretched himself flat along the wood: in vain. It was impossible to keep a hold on the grating as it tossed madly in the heavy sea.

It was a gruesome scene that met his eyes as Gödde, lifted on to the long crest of a wave, looked about him, a scene illuminated by starshell and the chalk-white beams of searchlights. Where their light met the blue-black ice-cold water it shone in flashes of dazzling silver. Gödde swam on slowly and steadily, his head turned towards the capsizing *Scharnhorst*. Through the whirling veil of great snowflakes he saw, garishly illuminated, the outline of the battleship now lying practically on her side. The sight seemed unreal, improbable. It flashed through his mind that a fighter plane, banking, would have seen the *Scharnhorst* like that. Everything was oblique, foreshortened, contradicting the laws of gravity. Only a few men were swimming on her starboard side, most of them having followed the advice of the Captain and left the *Scharnhorst* over the rail on

the port side. Later, after his rescue, Gödde thanked
Providence that he had gone overboard on the starboard side for nearly all the survivors had been picked
up on that side.

He saw the light of an emergency raft flickering close
to him. Uncannily, like a ship's distress signal, its flame
quivered restlessly in the gale. Gödde could see a young
officer and several men on the raft. He swam towards it
and saw the officer suddenly stand up. Through the
raging storm he heard him shout: "Three cheers for
the *Scharnhorst*!"

The P.O. and all who were swimming near joined in
the cheering. Gödde was now nearer to the raft, which
was drifting fairly close to the ship, and could already
recognize the faces of the men in the leaping light. Now
a young rating raised his arm:

"Three cheers for our families, our homeland!"

And again the cheers were taken up from all sides.
It was a soul-stirring moment which Gödde was never
to forget. From somewhere—as recounted later by
Sträter—came the sound of singing. Disjointed words,
half scattered by the wind, sounded across the water:

"On a sailor's tomb . . . no roses bloom . . ."

Two verses—then the song died away.

Suddenly Gödde heard shouts from several men who
were swimming closer to the ship:

"It's the Captain! He's swimming near the ship; he
can't hold out; he's got no life-jacket."

"Gödde knew then that the last man, the Captain,
had left the *Scharnhorst*. The last man, that is, who
could reach the upper deck. There were, he knew, many
who had not been able to get aloft. Among these was
the magazine personnel of the port IV 5·9-inch twin
turret and the men from the engine-rooms and from the
quarters below the armoured deck. And again came a

shout, clearly audible through the driving snow which, mingling now with hail, continued to fall in the yellow-white glare of starshell:

"Save the First Officer. He's swimming close to the ship and can't keep himself above water."

A swimmer near Gödde came closer and shouted something to him. He had to repeat it once or twice before Gödde understood:

"They both gave their life-jackets to men who had none!"

Gödde was two to three hundred yards from the ship which was now lying so much on her starboard side that he could look right down her funnel as into a dark tunnel. He was amazed that she was still afloat. He and many of his shipmates could still plainly hear the turbines revolving inside her. Fuel oil had spread across the sea, covering the surface with a tough, pungent, rainbow-coloured film. It was nauseating if it was washed into the mouth or even came into contact with the face. But, as Gödde quickly observed, it cushioned the violence of the breaking seas.

At the same time Sträter saw the *Scharnhorst* capsize and settle deeper into the water, bow first. All three propellers were still revolving at fair speed.

Gödde now tried to reach a raft which was drifting near him. Some twenty men were already sitting on it or clinging to it, so that, pressed below the surface by the combined weight of the men, nothing could be seen of the raft itself. Seeing this, Gödde abandoned his attempt and swam towards some wooden props such as were used by the damage control parties for propping up hatches, etc. They were drifting close together and when at last he reached them, they offered him some support. Of the ship's rafts only a few were in the water. Most of the rafts and life-boats had, on the Captain's orders, been cut free from their lashings in good time, but splinters and fragments of shell had riddled them with holes and rendered them useless. Clinging to the wooden props Gödde let himself drift about in the swell. Now he could relax sufficiently to look back to his ship; the *Scharnhorst* had turned turtle after capsizing and her superstructure, which Gödde had been able to see for so long, had disappeared. The wreck was drifting on the sea, bottom up, and men were moving about on the ship's keel, among them Artificer 1st Class Johnnie Merkel, one of the survivors. He remained perched on the keel until he saw a raft drifting by, then he jumped into the water. Sitting on the raft Merkel then helped several men over from the ship's bottom.

Meanwhile the cold began to take hold of Gödde; paralysis crept from his lower extremities and threatened to numb his whole body. Lumps of ice were drifting by, the snowstorm was still raging, and gusts of hail drove almost horizontally across the dark waters. Gödde was weakening. He had just reached the point when he felt he could keep his grip on the props no longer when he caught sight of the raft bearing Merkel and three other men. Summoning his last reserves Gödde managed to reach the raft. He let go of the props and Merkel helped the half-paralysed man to push the upper part of his body over on to the raft. Utterly exhausted Gödde cast a last glance back to the *Scharnhorst*. Only part of the stern was showing above the water. Then the long rolling swell of the Arctic sea closed over her.

Gradually the sound of starshell firing ceased and darkness reclaimed the sea. The little groups huddling on the few rafts could hardly see each other, still less the isolated swimmers. A young rating who had left his own raft because of overcrowding joined Gödde's company. He too was helped on by Merkel so that he could keep his hold by lying, like Gödde, with his body across the raft. They were all completely exhausted, incapable of feeling, half-numbed, stricken by a leaden weariness. For one to one and a half hours they drifted, the raft swinging up and down with the sea, floundering in monotonous rhythm between wave-crest and trough. Pressed tightly together, one supporting the other, they would, whenever the raft was lifted to the crest of an unusually high wave, look around them with eyes red-rimmed and swollen, encrusted with hoar-frost and caked with salt and oil.

Then, suddenly, they started: there was a flash quite near them, the thunder of guns broke loose again and the screaming of shells passed over their heads. Were they under fire? There came the sound of dull detonations, then the sky lit up around them. Flares shed their harsh light and a few seconds later the long white arms of searchlights pierced the darkness. For a moment the men thought that their raft was being fired on, then they realized their mistake. A great ship had concentrated her searchlights and was now spot-lighting the raft. In the light of starshell they saw two destroyers approach and stretch the thinner fingers of their searchlights too on to the raft, their raft. Then one of them turned away. The other continued towards them and, manœuvring cautiously, approached the raft. It struck Gödde, now fully conscious again, how skilfully the destroyer was managed in the heavy sea-way; she left the raft on her starboard side and then let herself drift with the wind towards it. Great climbing nets were laid out on the side of the destroyer and as soon as the vessel was close enough the British seamen threw bowlines over the heads and shoulders of the men on the raft. They were pulled on board one after another in this fashion. When Gödde had the sling thrown to him he had not the strength to slip it over his elbows, and as the British seaman went to pull him up he slipped out of the sling and back into the water. Four times they threw him the line: at the fifth attempt the end of the line hit him directly across the mouth. In desperation he sank his teeth firmly into the hemp rope and in this manner was hauled up. As he reached deck level he felt a pair of giant fists grasp the collar of his uniform and pull him over the rail.

The destroyer was the *Scorpion*. She rescued thirty *Scharnhorst* men; another destroyer, the *Matchless*, picked up six.

The British seamen cared for the German sailors in a way which—as Gödde reported—won their heartfelt gratitude. The sodden oil-soaked uniforms were at once removed and thrown overboard. The survivors were then taken to the mess-deck where the destroyer men made every effort to restore them with warm clothing and hot drinks and food. They learned that the British Battle Group to which this destroyer belonged—Force 2 —was to join the convoy and proceed to Murmansk.

Sträter, who with six other men drifted on his raft for about an hour and a half, was rescued by the same destroyer (*Scorpion*).

The next morning, 27 December 1943, the prisoners were taken singly to the First Officer for interrogation. They gave their personal particulars, and the valuables taken from them at the time of their rescue were returned to them. P.O. Gödde, as senior in rank and the only petty officer among the survivors, was asked certain more searching questions, but these he refused to answer.

In the afternoon of the same day, after passing Kola Inlet, the *Scorpion* anchored in Murmansk roads. Half an hour later the order came through for the prisoners to get ready and fall in on the upper deck. There each man received a duffle coat. A Russian tug then came alongside, to which the prisoners, guarded by British and Russian marines, had to transfer. They looked at each other in bewilderment. Were the English delivering them, German sailors, into the hands of the Russians? Why, they'd sooner jump overboard! The men grew restless.

The German-speaking British naval officer who was accompanying the transport went over to speak to the agitated men:

"Calm down! You're not being handed over to the Russians. The Commander-in-Chief has ordered that all *Scharnhorst* prisoners be taken on board the *Duke of York*. You will then be taken to England in the flagship."

Just before the tug drew alongside the battleship, which loomed out of the darkness like a massive fort, Johnnie Merkel, German-Canadian by birth, went up to the British destroyer officer, and speaking in English on behalf of his comrades, thanked the destroyer crew for their selfless care and solicitude. He concluded with the words:

"We all wish you a good voyage and a safe return home!"

Then he turned to his fellow survivors:

"My comrades of the *Scharnhorst*. Three cheers for the British destroyer men!"

All joined in. Gödde could not help thinking how strange it was. German cheers for British seamen in a Russian port. Loudly the cheers re-echoed from the high walls of the British battleship, a token of the eternal brotherhood between honest seamen the world over.

## XXI

## THE SURVIVORS OF THE
## *SCHARNHORST* ABOARD THE BRITISH
## FLAGSHIP *DUKE OF YORK*

(Report of P.O. Willi Gödde, survivor of the
*Scharnhorst*)

UPON release from captivity, P.O. Willi Gödde placed the following report at the disposal of his former First Officer Captain (retired) Giessler:

Arrived in the flagship, we first took our four seriously wounded men to the ship's sick-bay. Then we were taken to the quarters which were to accommodate us until we arrived in England. As senior in rank I was made responsible by the Commanding Officer of the Royal Marines for the order and cleanliness of our quarters.

Any requests on our part had to be referred to the interpreter, a young ship's doctor, with whom I had several long conversations. I put this question to him:

"What is your opinion of the battle and the sinking of the *Scharnhorst*? Could the sinking of our ship have been avoided?"

The English officer replied:

"Although actually I ought not to, I can tell you that after the action Admiral Sir Bruce Fraser called the ship and staff officers together and said: 'Gentlemen: The battle against the *Scharnhorst* has ended in victory for us. I hope that if any of you are ever called upon to lead a ship into action against an opponent many times superior, you will command your ship as gallantly as the *Scharnhorst* was commanded today.'

I have nothing to add to these words of our Commander-in-Chief. But please keep this to yourself for the moment; you can tell your friends later on. And now I have to inform you that the Commander-in-Chief wishes to see the survivors this afternoon at three o'clock. Would you therefore have your men ready at that time? As senior in rank you will have to give the commands. Have them stand to attention and give the proper salute according to German routine. Suitable clothing will be provided."

We were accordingly issued with striped civilian trousers, blue jerseys and slippers. We also received shaving kit and combs so that we could put up a good appearance.

Shortly before 1500 hours I had the men fall in. Punctually at 1500 hours bugles sounded through the ship and the British Commander-in-Chief entered our room with his staff. I gave the command and we saluted. The British Admiral took up his stance about three feet in front of our ranks, his officers behind him. The Commander-in-Chief raised his hand to his cap and all the officers, among them the Captain of the *Duke of York*, followed his example. For a full minute they honoured thus in silence their vanquished opponents. We all realized that this mark of respect applied not to us personally, but to our proud ship and her gallant dead.

Then Admiral Fraser reviewed each rank—because of the restricted space we were drawn up five ranks deep—and, accompanied by an interpreter, talked to practically every man, asking him his age, profession, where he lived, why he had joined the navy, etc.

Finally he stepped in front again and said:

"We honour a brave opponent even if he has been

beaten. The British people harbour no hatred against you. Have no misgivings about being taken to England. Just do as you are told and you will be all right."

We repeated our salute, the British Commander-in-Chief and his officers returned it and left the room. Never shall I forget the solemnity of that moment.

The next day we had to present ourselves again when we received a visit from the ship's Captain and officers. The Captain told me on this occasion that the Commander-in-Chief had ordered that the prisoners were to be well treated and were to have the same food, etc. as the crew. We were to be given every possible comfort.

During the passage from Murmansk to Scapa Flow we were allowed to exercise on the upper deck and between the aircraft-hangars and were much photographed by war reporters and members of the crew. We were given excellent treatment the whole time we were in the *Duke of York*. Six men of the Royal Marines acted as guards, and after some initial reticence, we were soon on friendly terms with them.

I should mention that in Murmansk, when we were taken on board the *Duke of York*, and during the passage, we saw welding repairs being carried out in this ship and in other large units. As our quarters on the lower deck were placed about midships and we had to pass several compartments many times a day on our way to the wash-room and toilets on the battery deck, we were able to confirm that the ship had many battle scars, some of them quite considerable, as for instance the torn bows between the battery and the lower deck. I asked the English doctor, our interpreter, if the ship had received any direct hits.

"That, of course, I must not tell you," he replied. "But one thing I will say: we hadn't a dry spot anywhere on the battery and lower decks. We had to keep the electric and hand pumps going day and night. Does that satisfy you?"

For six whole days and nights after our rescue I could not sleep. No sedative prescribed by the doctor had any effect. Only after putting into Scapa Flow did I sleep for two or three hours aboard an old patrol vessel. Our own men behaved splendidly, each seeking to help the other. Eventually we were separated in London where we had to pass through several interrogation camps. Eight men later went to Canada and twenty-seven to the United States. Sträter, I heard later, was exchanged.

On the occasion of a lecture to members of former *Scharnhorst* crews in Wilhelmshaven, Gödde mentioned another chivalrous gesture on the part of the British.

On the return from Murmansk a great wreath was dropped from the *Duke of York* at the spot where the German battleship had gone down. It was announced in German through the flagship's loudspeaker system that the ceremony was to honour the brave crew of the *Scharnhorst*.

Gödde's remarks on the damage observed in the *Duke of York* may be qualified by details from the dispatch of the British Commander-in-Chief:

Sir Bruce says that the *Duke of York* lay for an hour and a half under the entire heavy fire of the enemy. She was, to quote the Admiral, "frequently straddled by near misses ahead, astern and on the beam. Both masts were shot through by 11-inch shell which fortunately did not explode. No direct hits were scored" (i.e. only splinters).

# XXII

## COMPARISON OF THE FORCES
## PARTICIPATING IN THE BATTLE

IT is notable that the *Scharnhorst*—like the *Bismarck* two years before—could not be defeated by gun-fire. In the last analysis she was sunk by torpedoes (56 were fired at her in the course of the action, and 14 or 15 hits were scored), and after scuttling herself in accordance with the German Navy's instructions for such an emergency.

In spite of these heavy torpedo hits, and the hits of the *Duke of York's* heavy guns, the ship's engines were working perfectly to the very end. Right to the last she had electric current and the Damage Control Officers and their teams were able to localize the effects of hits and maintain safety on board. In this connexion special mention should be made of the Chief Engineer, Korvettenkapitän Otto König, the Electrical Engineer, Korvettenkapitän v. Glass, and the two Damage Control Officers, Kapitänleutnant Därr and Oberleutnant Timmer, and all their technical personnel.

The superiority of the forces that, through the outstanding leadership of the British Commander-in-Chief, Admiral Sir Bruce Fraser, were concentrated against the *Scharnhorst* during the last half-hour of the action of 26 December 1943 can best be illustrated by contrasting the participating forces and their armament. The following comparison was tabulated by Captain (retired) Giessler and is quoted with his permission.

## COMPLEMENTS

German complement:
    Approx. 1,900 men.

British complements:
    Force 1 : approx.   2,930 men
    Force 2 : approx.   3,400 men

    Total: approx.   6,330 men

## ARMAMENT

*Scharnhorst:*
    9—11-inch
    12—5·9-inch
    14—4·1-inch A.A.
    6 torpedo tubes.

Force 1
    8—8-inch
    21—6-inch
    20—4·7-inch
    28—4-inch A.A.
    2—3-inch A.A.
    20 torpedo tubes

Force 2
    10—14-inch
    12—6-inch
    16—5·25-inch
    8—4-inch A.A.
    38 torpedo tubes

Total
    10—14-inch
    8—8-inch
    33—6-inch
    16—5·25-inch
    20—4·7-inch
    36—4-inch A.A.
    2—3-inch A.A.
    58 torpedo tubes

# BIBLIOGRAPHY

Dispatch of the Flottenkommando dated 6 October 1944.

Dr Curt Bley: *Geheimnis Radar, "Die Welt"*, 1949 (concerning the discovery of the "Rotterdam apparatus").

*Brassey's Naval Annual 1948*, William Clowes & Sons (Führer Conferences and Naval Affairs).

Viscount Cunningham of Hyndhope: *A Sailor's Odyssey*, Hutchinson, London, 1951.

C. S. Forester: *Saturday Evening Post*, 25 March 1944. (Report on the Sinking of the *Scharnhorst*.)

Admiral Lord Fraser, Earl of Northcape, Dispatch on the Sinking of the *Scharnhorst*, *London Gazette*, Supplement 38038.

Helmuth Giessler: *Kriegstagebuch*.

Handbuch für die West und Nordküste Norwegens, II Teil (Von Drontheim bis zur norwegish-finnischen Grenze), 1939, Deutsches Hydrographisches Institut, Hamburg (Nachtrag 1949/50).

Anthony Martienssen: *Hitler and his Admirals*, Secker & Warburg, London, 1948.

Sir W. M. James: *The British Navies in the Second World War*, Longmans, Green, London, 1947.

Karl Peter: *Schlachkreuzer Scharnhorst*, E. S. Mittler & Son, Darmstadt, 1951 (concerning the Reconnaissance wireless signals of U-boats and aircraft, and the exchange of wireless signals with the 4th Destroyer Flotilla).

The author is greatly indebted to Captain (retired) Helmuth Giessler, former Navigating and First Officer of the *Scharnhorst*, who put at his disposal important material such as the reports of the German Flottenkommando, the Dispatch of the British Commander-in-Chief, newspaper reports, maritime and battle charts. Captain Giessler also read the manuscript and gave the author the benefit of his years of experience on board the *Scharnhorst*.

M

The description of the experiences of the three captains of the 5th Mine-Sweeper Flotilla, R 56, R 58 and R 121 is based on an interview with the Captain of R 58, Lieutenant (retired) Werner Hauss, who kindly placed his reminiscences at the author's disposal.

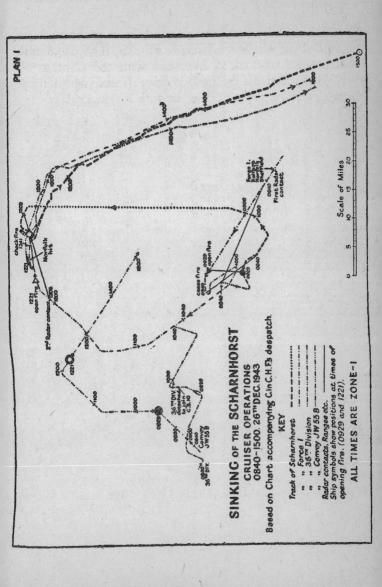

PLAN I

# SINKING of the SCHARNHORST
## CRUISER OPERATIONS
## 0840–1500. 26ᵀᴴ DEC. 1943
Based on Chart accompanying C.in C.H.F.'s despatch.
### KEY

Track of Scharnhorst ————————
" " Force 1 — — — — —
" " 36ᵀᴴ Division —··—··—··—
" " Convoy JW 55 B ————————
Radar contacts, Ranges etc. ————————
Ship symbols show positions at times of
opening fire. (0929 and 1221).

**ALL TIMES ARE ZONE–1**

Scale of Miles
0    5    10    15    20    25    30

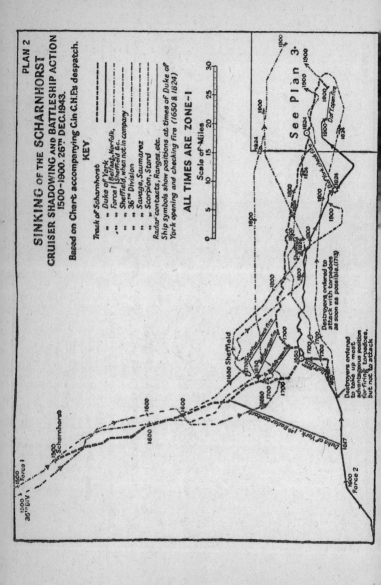

PLAN 2

# SINKING OF THE SCHARNHORST
## CRUISER SHADOWING AND BATTLESHIP ACTION
### 1500–1900. 26TH DEC.1943.

Based on Chart accompanying C.in C.H.F's despatch.

KEY

Track of Scharnhorst
    " Duke of York,
    " Force I Belfast, Norfolk,
    " Sheffield &c.
    " Sheffield, when not in company
    " 36ᵗʰ Division
    " Savage, Saumarez
    " Scorpion, Stord

Radar contacts, Ranges, etc.
Ship symbols show positions at times of
Duke of York opening and checking fire (1650 & 1624)

ALL TIMES ARE ZONE–I

Scale of Miles

0   5   10   15   20   25   30

See Plan 3.

Duke of York open fire

Destroyers, ordered to attack with torpedoes as soon as possible.(1713)

Destroyers ordered to take up most advantageous position for firing torpedoes, but not to attack.

Duke of York 1st Radar Contact

1647

1900 Force 2

Sheffield

Duke of York check fire

Sheffield check fire

1650 Sheffield

1500 36ᵗʰ DIV. 1500 Force I
Scharnhorst

PLAN 3

SINKING OF THE SCHARNHORST
1845-1945  26TH DEC. 1943

KEY

| | |
|---|---|
| Track of Scharnhorst | — — — |
| " Duke of York | ———— |
| " Jamaica (when detached) | — · — |
| " Savage, Saumarez | — · · — |
| " Scorpion, Stord | — ··· — |
| " Force I, Belfast & Norfolk | — ·· — |
| " Sheffield | — — |
| " 36th Division | — ·· — |
| " Virago, Opportune (when detached, | |
| " Musketeer, Matchless (detached) | |
| Ranges, etc. | |

ALL TIMES ARE ZONE -1

Scale of Miles

0  1  2  3  4  5  6  7  8  9  10

# INDEX

*Acanthus*, corvette, 81
*Acasta*, destroyer, 13, 28
*Admiral Hipper*, heavy cruiser, 21, 22, 23, 24, 25, 26, 27, 32, 46
*Admiral Scheer*, pocket battleship, 32, 41, 46
*Adria*, tanker, 32
Akureyri, 79, 83
Alta Fjord, 41, 46, 51, 54, 55–6, 88, 119
*Ardent*, destroyer, 13, 28
*Ashanti*, destroyer, 81
*Athabascan*, destroyer, 81

*Beagle*, destroyer, 81
Bear Island, 48, 53, 80, 84, 85, 86, 89, 98
Behr, Kapitänleutnant, 64
*Belfast*, light cruiser, 81, 90, 107, 108, 126, 132, 138, 143, 160, 161, 162
Berlin, 76–7
*Bernd von Arnim*, destroyer, 22
Bey, Rear-Admiral, Acting C.-in-C. 1st Battle Group, 46, 49–50, 51, 54, 60, 65, 78, 96–7, 98, 99, 100, 101, 109, 110, 111, 112–13, 116–17, 118–20, 121, 148, 149, 155, 157, 158
Birkle, Able Seaman, 151
*Bismarck*, battleship, 34, 35, 175
Bley, Dr Curt, *The Radar Secret*, 76
Bosse, Oberleutnant, 149, 155–6
Bredenbreuker, Korvettenkapitän, 111, 113, 117, 134, 135, 136, 159
Brest, 13, 34, 35, 36
Burnett, Vice-Admiral, 81, 84, 87, 90, 107, 108, 126, 127, 129, 130, 131

Cherbourg, 37
Cherwell, Lord, 77
Ciliax, Vice-Admiral, 11, 16, 36, 37, 38, 39
Clouston, Lt-Commander, 82
*Convoys*
  J.W. 55A, 79, 80
  J.W. 55B, 48, 80, 81, 84, 85, 86, 89
  R.A. 55A, 48, 80, 86, 89

Därr, Kapitänleutnant, 175
Deierling, Bo'sun's Mate, 163–4
*Dianella*, corvette, 81
*Dithmarschen*, supply ship, 26
Dominik, Fregattenkapitän, 61–3, 66–7, 99, 148, 149, 150, 157, 159, 166
Dönitz, Grand-Admiral, 43, 45, 46, 48, 49, 93–4, 97
*Duke of York*, battleship, 79, 82, 83, 85, 87, 90, 122, 126, 129, 130, 132, 138, 142, 159, 160, 161, 162, 170, 171–4, 175
Dunkelberg, Oberleutnant zur See, 93, 97

Eastern Front, 45
Eisenbart, U-boat Flotilla, 53, 94, 122
English Channel, break-through, 36–40
Eya Fjord, 83

Fraser, Admiral Sir Bruce, 79, 80, 81–2, 83, 84, 85, 86, 87, 88, 89, 90, 96, 108, 122, 126, 127, 129–130, 131, 138, 139, 141, 159, 162, 171–3 174, 175
Fügner, Kapitänleutnant, 153
Führer Conference, December 1943, 46
*Furious*, aircraft-carrier, 25

Giessler, Captain Helmuth, 11, 15–16, 22–3, 37, 171, 175, 177
*Gleaner*, minesweeper, 81
*Glorious*, aircraft-carrier, 13, 28
*Gneisenau*, battleship, 13, 14, 15, 16, 17, 18, 19, 21, 23, 25, 26, 27, 29, 31, 33, 34, 35, 39, 40, 41, 46
Gödde, Oberbootsmannsmaat, Acting C.P.O., 67, 103–4, 105, 114, 115–16, 117–18, 124–5, 133, 134–6, 137, 140–1, 144, 145–6, 147, 148, 155, 157, 159, 162, 163–9, 170, 171–4
Göring, Hermann, 76
Goss, Midshipman, 27
Gotenhaven, 31, 41, 46
*Graf Spee*, battleship, 28
Grimsey Island, 83

184

*Haida*, destroyer, 81
Hammerfest, 51, 54, 69, 70
Hansen, Kapitänleutnant, 54
Harstad, 26, 27
Hauss, Sub-Lieutenant Werner, 55,
    56–7, 58, 59–65, 67–8, 70, 178
*Hermann Schoemann*, destroyer, 77
Heye, Captain, 25
Hintze, Captain, 60, 61, 62, 67, 78,
    92, 93–6, 97, 98, 99, 101, 106,
    111–13, 114, 116, 118–20, 124,
    133, 134, 135–6, 137, 145–6, 147,
    148–9, 153, 154, 155, 157–8, 159,
    163, 165
Hoffmann, Captain Curt Caesar, 16,
    17, 18, 19, 21, 22–3, 24, 27, 28,
    30, 41
*Honeysuckle*, corvette, 81
*Huaskaran*, repair ship, 30
Hüffmeier, Captain, 41
Hughes-Hallet, Captain, 82
*Huron*, destroyer, 81

*Impulse*, destroyer, 81
*Iroquois*, destroyer, 81

Jade, River, 16, 17, 20
*Jamaica*, light cruiser, 79, 82, 83,
    131, 132, 138, 142, 159, 160, 161,
    162
Jan Mayen Island, 24, 84
Johannesson, Captain, 96, 101, 110,
    120–1, 123
Jürgens, Chief Quartermaster, 52,
    113
Jutland, 20

Kaa Fjord, 46, 51, 69, 124
Kaiser-Wilhelm Canal, 16–17
Kennedy, Captain E. C., 19
Kiel, 17, 20, 26, 31, 40
Kola Bay, 79
Kola Inlet, 79, 126, 162, 169
König, Korvettenkapitän Otto, 61,
    175
Kummertz, Admiral, 46

Lang Fjord, 41, 51, 55–6, 58, 66,
    67, 69
Lanz, Korvettenkapitän, 97, 112,
    119, 157
La Pallice, 14, 35
Lappahavet, 70, 93
Liebhardt, Chief Engineer, 29
Lofoten Islands, 23
Lübsen, Kapitänleutnant, 109, 110,
    111, 120
Luftwaffe, 14, 26, 36, 40, 43, 45

Lütjens, Admiral, 31, 32, **33**
*Lützow*, 46

Maclot, Leutnant Wilhelm, 55, 56,
    59–65, 67–8, 70
*Malaya*, battleship, 33
Marschall, Vice-Admiral, 17, 18, 21,
    25, 26, 27
*Matchless*, destroyer, 81, 89, 108,
    160, 161, 162, 169
Merkel, Artificer 1st Class Johnnie,
    167, 170
*Meteor*, destroyer, 81
Meyrick, Commander, 82
*Milne*, destroyer, 81
Moritz, Chief Gunner, C.P.O., 106,
    151, 152, 155
Murmansk, 35, 42, 46, 47, 73, 79,
    81, 86, 169
*Musketeer*, destroyer, 80–1, 89, 108,
    127, 138, 160

Narvik, 23, 26, 27
Narvik Group, 21, 23, 25
*Newcastle*, cruiser, 19
Nordmann, Admiral, 52
*Norfolk*, heavy cruiser, 81, 90, 107,
    108, 126, 127, 132, 138, 160, 162
North Cape, 47, 48, 80, 112, 114,
    123
North Friesian islands, 17
Norway and Denmark, occupation
    of, 21, 24

*Onslaught*, destroyer, 81
*Onslow*, destroyer, 81
*Opportune*, destroyer, 80–1, 89,
    108, 160, 161
*Orwell*, destroyer, 81
*Oxlip*, corvette, 81

Peter, Karl, *Schlachtkreuzer Scharn-
    horst*, 113–14
Pietz, Leading Signalman, 70
Plate, River, 28
Point Lucie, 55, 70, 93, 121, 124
*Poppy*, corvette, 81
*Prinz Eugen*, 14, 35, 39, 46

R 56, minesweeper, 55, 56, 58, 65–
    66, 68, 69, 70
R 58, minesweeper, 55, 56, 58, 65–
    66, 68, 69, 70
R 121, minesweeper, 65, 68, 69
Radar, 17, 26, 36, 45, 76–8, 92, 95,
    98, 100, 104, 105, 106–7, 108,
    109, 115, 119, 122, 126, 129–30,
    132, 133, 141, 159

*Ramillies*, battleship, 33
*Rawalpindi*, auxiliary cruiser, 13, 19
*Renown*, 24
Roth, Generalleutnant, Air Officer Commanding North-west, 114
"Rotterdam apparatus", 76 (see also Radar)
Royal Air Force, 13, 14, 30, 34
Russell, Capt. the Hon. G H. E. 82, 83, 85, 132, 172, 173

*Saumarez*, destroyer, 79, 138, 142
*Savage*, destroyer, 79, 138, 142
Scapa Flow, 26, 31
Schären, 30, 123, 124
*Scharnhorst I*, armoured cruiser of World War I, 15
*Scharnhorst*, battleship,
  laid down, 1935, 16
  launched, 16
  commissioned 1939, 11
  trials, 16
  equipped with Radar at Kiel, 17
  first offensive sweep, 17–20
  action against *Rawalpindi*, 18-19
  exercises in Baltic, 20
  sortie to Stavanger, 20
  occupation of Norway and Denmark, 21–5
  action off Lofoten Islands, 23–4
  sights *Renown*, 23–4
  Narvik operation, 26–9
  operation against convoys, 27
  action against *Glorious*, 28–9
  hit, puts into Trondhjem, 29–30
  ordered to Stavanger, 30–31
  Kiel, dockyard refitting, 31
  attacks merchant shipping in North Atlantic, 32–4
  at Brest and La Pallice, 13–14, 34–5
  Channel break-through, 1942, 14, 36–40
  offensive sweep to Spitsbergen, 41
  ordered to attack Murmansk convoy, 48
  puts to sea, 67
  receives W/T message from Grand Admiral, 94
  encounter with Cruiser Squadron, Force 1, 103–7
  second encounter with Cruiser Squadron, Force 1, 109–118, 126–7
  action against *Duke of York*, 121–122, 132, 134–7
  attacked by destroyer sub-division, Force 2, 139–42

*Scharnhorst* (continued)
  second action against *Duke of York*, 144–53
  torpedo attack by British destroyers, 154–6, 159–62
  Captain orders Abandon Ship, 157–9
  capsizes, 166
  sinks, 14, 167
  rescue of survivors, 163–70
Schniewind, Admiral, 49, 54
Schreck, First Lieutenant, 24
Schrewe, First Lieutenant, 24
*Scorpion*, destroyer, 79, 138, 142, 162, 169
*Scourge*, destroyer, 81
*Seagull*, minesweeper, 81
*Sheffield*, light cruiser, 81, 90, 108, 126, 127, 128, 138, 162
Shetland Isles, 17, 22, 25
Skagen, 26
Skagerrak, 21, 26
Söröya Island, 55
Spitzbergen, 41, 47, 48
Spitzbergen Group, 80
Stadlandet, Cape, 19
Stalingrad, 42
Stavanger, 20, 30, 31
Stjern Sund, 69, 70, 93
Stobka, Chief Quartermaster Horst, 65
Stoeroey Sund, 70, 93
*Stord*, destroyer, 79, 138, 142
Storehill, Lt.-Commander, 82
Sträter, Ordinary Seaman 1st Class Günter, 97, 105, 125, 134, 150, 151, 155, 165, 166, 169, 174

*Telefunken* Company, 76
Terschelling, 40
*Times, The*, 40
Timmer, Oberleutnant, 175
*Tirpitz*, battleship, 41, 45–6, 51, 54, 60, 65, 67, 124
Tromsoe, 27, 51, 114
Trondhjem, 24, 26, 27, 29, 53
Trondhjem Fjord, 23, 30

Utsire, Isle of, 30

Varget Sund, 69
Versailles, Treaty of, 16
*Virago*, destroyer, 81, 89, 108, 160, 161
Voith-Schneider type vessel, 55, 57
von Glass, Korvettenkapitän, 175

Walmsley, Lt.-Commander, 82
*Westcott*, destroyer, 81
Western Approaches Command, 79, 81
West Fjord, 23, 41
West Wall, mine-belt, 17
*Whitehall*, destroyer, 81
Wibbelhoff, Staff Chief-Gunner, 106, 140, 152, 154–5
Wieting, Kapitänleutnant, 117, 135, 144, 152, 159

Wilhelmshaven, 16, 25, 40
Wolfsschanze, 46
*Wrestler*, destroyer, 81

Z 26, destroyer, 77
Z 29, destroyer, 51, 68, 70, 99, 100, 101, 109, 110, 111, 123
Z 30, destroyer, 51, 100, 120
Z 33, destroyer, 51, 121, 124
Z 34, destroyer, 51, 68
Z 38, destroyer, 51, 68, 101

# WHEN THE MOON RISES

## TONY DAVIES

A trainload of British prisoners of war steams
slowly through the Italian mountains.
Suddenly there is a screeching of brakes and
the sound of shots from the guards. Two
British officers have made the leap for
freedom . . .

Tony Davies's first escape bid ends in
recapture and transfer to a new camp in the
north. When he escapes again he and his
companions are faced with a 700 mile walk
along the spine of the Appenines to the Allied
beach-head at Salerno. The journey begins as
a schoolboy adventure: it ends as a terrifying
and deadly game of hide-and-seek where
the Germans hunt down the fugitives like
animals and courageous Italian peasants risk
their own lives to save them.

# ESCAPE FROM THE RISING SUN
# IAN SKIDMORE

'The oily dust fell everywhere, on hungry stragglers searching for their units, on armed deserters who roamed the streets searching for loot, on . . . fear-crazed men fighting their way at the point of a gun or bayonet, pushing women and children aside . . . The dead lay in the streets . . . but no one collected the corpses now.'

Singapore had fallen. The British Army, retreating in disorder before the onslaught of the Japanese shock-troops, had been told to surrender. One man was convinced he could escape.

Geoffrey Rowley-Conwy seized a junk and sailed for Padang. There he joined a group of fellow officers for a desperate escape-bid in a dilapidated sailing boat across the Indian Ocean to Ceylon. 1,500 miles of open sea swept by the fury of the monsoon and patrolled by Japanese fighter planes on the lookout for British survivors.

'One of the best and liveliest escape stories of the Second World War . . . enthralling.'
Times Literary Supplement

# VIZZINI

# THE SECRET LIFE OF AMERICA'S NO. 1 UNDERCOVER AGENT BY SAL VIZZINI

In the course of his extraordinary career Sal Vizzini was shot three times, knifed twice, savagely beaten up and has had several contracts put out by the Mafia to kill him.

His story packs into one book enough material for a whole series of novels. As an undercover agent for the F.B.I., he was assigned to Naples where he became a 'friend' of exiled Mafia chieftain Charles 'Lucky' Luciano; to Burma, where he blew up a heroin factory; to Lebanon, where he outwitted a Communist gun-running ring; and to Atlanta, Georgia, where he posed as a con in the Federal Pen in order to find out where a million dollars in government bonds had been hidden by a prisoner.

# The Reluctant Musketeer

# Anthony Burton

## A Story of National Service

2763418 Aircraftman Second Class Grant had no ambitions to come top of the class, win promotion or, God forbid, win any medals. He just wanted to survive his National Service stint as painlessly as he could.

The accommodating Rita, nicknamed the camp bicycle ("because everyone rode her"), certainly helped to ease the pain; as did Mavis and Cynthia, the baton twirling, hip swaying drum majorettes of the Calgary High School Band.

Unfortunately Grant also had a talent for getting himself into trouble. His two years with the RAF turned into a riot of misadventures with the randy Irishman Paddy Ferguson, the incurable air-sick Ellie and the lunatic Eric Wade who took to dressing in women's clothes to prove he wasn't queer. It took them from the frozen prairies of Canada to the blistering heat of Cyprus . . . and finally to the ludicrous climax of the Suez War, codename Operation Musketeer.

# SS

# SS PANZER BATTALION LEO KESSLER

JANUARY 1940 . . . the coldest winter within living memory and the phoney war still paralyses the Western front. But at the Adolf Hitler Kaserne, a new battalion of SS troops trains for a mission so secret that it is known only by its WEHRMACHT code name, ZERO.

THE VULTURE – Major Horst Geier – is the only man who knows that the objective is the key Belgian fortress guarding the junction of the River Meuse and the Albert Canal – the most impregnable fort in Europe, which must be taken regardless of the cost in human lives if Hitler's hand-picked SS Panzer troops are to turn the flank of the Maginot Line.

SS PANZER BATTALION is the first novel in a new series about ASSAULT REGIMENT WOTAN, a crack unit in the Waffen SS.

# THOR HEYERDAHL
## Sea Routes to Polynesia

## WHO WERE THE POLYNESIANS?

When Thor Heyerdahl first suggested that the Polynesian Islands could have been colonised in prehistoric times by South American Indians who crossed the Pacific on wooden rafts, many of the experts remained sceptical. How, they asked, could the frail reed and balsa wood rafts of the South American Indians have spanned such enormous distances?

The *Kon-Tiki* expedition proved that it was possible: now, in *Sea Routes to Polynesia*, Thor Heyerdahl explores the theories behind his epic voyage, describes his subsequent discoveries and provides a fascinating insight into the islands, peoples and customs of the Pacific from the Malay peninsular to the coast of Ecuador, from the aborigines of the Galapagos to the statues of Rano-Raraku on Easter Island.